You're On Your Own

(BUT I'M HERE IF YOU NEED ME)

MENTORING YOUR CHILD

DURING THE

COLLEGE YEARS

Marjorie Savage

3rd Edition

TOUCHSTONE

New York   London   Toronto   Sydney   New Delhi

TOUCHSTONE
An Imprint of Simon & Schuster, Inc.
1230 Avenue of the Americas
New York, NY 10020

This Touchstone paperback edition May 2020

TOUCHSTONE and colophon are trademarks of Simon & Schuster, Inc.

For information about special discounts for bulk purchases, please contact Simon & Schuster Special Sales at 1-866-506-1949 or business@simonandschuster.com.

The Simon & Schuster Speakers Bureau can bring authors to your live event. For more information or to book an event, contact the Simon & Schuster Speakers Bureau at 1-866-248-3049 or visit our website at www.simonspeakers.com.

Manufactured in the United States of America

1   3   5   7   9   10   8   6   4   2

The Library of Congress Cataloging-in-Publication data has been applied for.

ISBN 978-1-9821-3653-6
ISBN 978-1-4391-6628-4 (ebook)

TO ALL PARENTS, FAMILY MEMBERS, FRIENDS,
AND SUPPORTERS OF COLLEGE-BOUND STUDENTS:
RELAX. YOU WILL STILL BE FAMILY
LONG AFTER THE COLLEGE YEARS.

Acknowledgments

To my colleagues across the country who work with parents and families of college students: you are the most generous, patient, thoughtful, creative, hilarious, and kind women and men in existence. There is not enough space on this page to name all of you, so I will do my best to thank you individually.

I owe special acknowledgments to my friends in higher education who helped with this book: Jodi Dworkin, Tina Falkner, Antonia Lortis, Paul Timmins, Amelious Whyte, Deanie Kepler, Chelsea Petree, Heather Pearson, Sara Nagle Newberg, and Kari Erpenbach. I am grateful for your time, knowledge, and advice.

A book doesn't get published just because someone writes it. To my literary agent, Betsy Amster: this book is the result of your encouragement and persistence.

The book is better because of Deb Parker's keen eye. Thank you, Deb.

For their enduring friendship and wisdom, I salute the Manifesto Ladies.

Most important, to my own family, Devor, Christine, Noah, and Kat: thank you for all the love and laughter.

Contents

Introduction

College is more expensive, complex, and consequential today than ever before.

Without a college education, a young adult's job options are limited, and wages are minimal. But a college degree requires a major financial investment. The average sticker price for just one year at a public university starts at about $25,000; at an elite private college, the cost can be three times that amount.

It's not just the expense, though. Life changes significantly when the family focus turns to college. For the student, the years of preparing for and attending college can feel like an unending series of life-altering decisions, transitions, and unpredictable events. For family members, this stage of parenting calls for new ways of guiding and supporting their child.

That's why parents start saving for college when their children are still toddlers. That's why families begin scheduling campus tours long before their children can fill out their first applications. That's why parents and students stay connected, not just during the college search, but throughout the entire college experience.

Since their children's first day of preschool, parents have been advised to be involved. "Know their teachers, know their friends, know what they're doing and who they're doing it with." From kindergarten through high school graduation, schools fostered parent involvement by sending weekly—or even daily—updates on classroom activities. Part of a parent's nightly routine was to check the school's online portal and respond to any notes from the teachers.

That family involvement has built strong family ties. Today's college freshmen identify their parents as their best advisers and turn to them first when they need help, or when they just want someone to talk to. Meanwhile, technology has made it easier for family members to stay in touch, with options for quick text check-ins, emails for messages that don't need an immediate response, and FaceTime calls that provide visual contact.

The purpose of this book is to help families navigate the college years and recognize the typical issues and developmental stages of young adulthood. The book identifies resources for students and their families, and it offers suggestions on when parents might need to step in to help their student and when to empower the student to take responsibility.

In these pages, families will find real-life examples of college and family issues, such as

- Working with your student during the college selection process
- Coping with the mood changes of the entire family during the months leading up to move-in day on campus
- Understanding student development during the college years
- Recognizing illnesses common among college-aged students and helping your child stay healthy
- Teaching students to manage their finances

- Using this time of change as an opportunity to expand your own horizons
- Preparing for the challenges most likely to emerge as your student navigates all four years of college
- Handling the transitions you and your student will face after college graduation

The book is written for parents, grandparents, aunts, uncles, siblings, family friends, and all others who play a prominent role in supporting a college student. The words "parent" and "family" are used to represent any and all who stand as caregivers or trusted supporters for a college student. Many examples in the book are attributed as the experience of a male or female, but in nearly every case, they could happen to a student or parent of any gender.

No family will experience all the situations described in these pages. The information includes advice and suggestions for families of traditional 18- to 22-year-old students who live on campus, as well as families of commuter students, transfer students, first-generation college students, students with disabilities, families of color, and international families.

The book is presented in four sections, starting with "The Path to College." This section describes the college search and ideas for beginning the transfer of responsibilities from parent to student. The second section, "Early Days," examines the student's initial transition to campus. It includes information about what the rest of the family experiences when a student starts college. Section three, "College Culture," offers insights into campus life, with examples of how families can support their student's academic, financial, social, and physical development. The last section, "Focus on the Future," looks at students' increasing levels of independence as they move into a first apartment, develop career plans, and graduate to jobs and adulthood. Each chapter concludes with a list of Quick Tips for Students that can be passed along to students.

The material comes from my own years of working in student affairs, parent/family services, and family development, and from the experiences of my colleagues throughout the country. The examples cited are from real-life interactions with college families, although names and identities have been changed to protect student privacy.

During the college years, parents and their children are developing a new, adult relationship—one based on love and respect—that will last a lifetime. As mothers, fathers, and other supporters move away from closely monitoring a student's daily activities, they begin to take on the role of mentor.

Mentoring is a concept that students, families, and educators can all embrace. With roots in mythology, the word has come to mean trusted adviser and counselor. It allows respect for a student's individuality and personal responsibility, and it defines a valid and vital role for parents as partners with colleges on behalf of their students.

SECTION 1
The Path to College

CHAPTER 1

Endless Possibilities

The College Search

When parents and prospective students arrive on campus for a college tour, they study the scenery as they make their way to the admissions office. "Is that a professor?" they wonder, seeing a man wearing jeans and a sport coat. "Students," they think as they sidestep a pair of young adults walking together, both silently studying their phones. "This must be the place," they decide, spotting a welcome banner over a pathway lined with flowers and flags in the school's colors.

Your family's first campus visit represents a major action step in your child's future. You may have been saving for years, and you've imagined delivering your son or daughter to a sun-drenched, ivy-covered campus someday in the distant future. Now you're planning college tours and talking with your teenager about goals, dreams, and an eventual career. You're focused on finding the best value for your investment and the best collegiate experience for your child.

For many high school students, though, nothing seems more intimidating than the responsibility of choosing a college. Despite the fact that there are some four thousand colleges and universities in the United States, for a teenager facing the college decision, it feels as though there are only two possibilities: the one, elusive *right* school and all the wrong ones.

Some families survive the college search with no scars, but most experience at least a few serious battles along the way. One father complained that his daughter's college search had barely started, and already the whole family was on edge.

"I was looking forward to this 'emerging adult' stage in Zoë's life, but every time the subject of college comes up, she ends up teary and angry. Her only plan is to move to New York and study cello at Juilliard. Did she have to pick the most selective music program in the country? She's talented, but really, her chances of getting into Juilliard are pretty slim. She's in one of those 'I know more than you' stages. I have no idea how to handle this without making it sound like I don't believe in her."

At least his daughter had a school in mind. That's a starting point. For many high school students, the idea of narrowing that list of four thousand to just a handful can be daunting. They're told by their high school counselors to look for schools that offer the major they want; then they're told they will probably change their major two or three times before they graduate. They're advised to come up with an initial list of schools, including some that could be a stretch to get into and a few that will be a sure bet. But how do you choose? And why not dream big and apply to *all* the top schools?

One thorough and resourceful student developed a comprehensive list of thirty. She included six dream schools; five that would be a reach but could be possible; several third- and fourth-place choices; and five that she knew she could get into but really didn't want to attend. Then her parents added up the numbers and advised her that applying to all those colleges would cost two thousand dollars in application fees.

When students begin their college search, they're jumping into a whirlwind of consumer marketing. They start by going to websites with slick search engines that will match them to the "best college for you!" They select their preferences for a major, a geographical area, and their interests and hobbies. Soon they're getting glossy publications, enthusiastic texts and email messages, and phone calls from admissions staff on a daily basis. They check the links to online videos hosted by college students who rave about their dorm rooms, favorite classes, and quirky but lovable roommates. Meanwhile friends, relatives, teachers, and high school counselors suggest even more colleges to "at least think about."

It's hard for family members to understand the pressure their child is feeling. For parents, the college search has a logical sequence, neatly arranged into basic steps:

- Scan the options; gather information.
- Compare and assess the possibilities based on choice of major, cost, and location.
- Draw up a short list for further comparisons.
- Apply; wait for decisions.
- Select a school.

Getting your student to follow that sequence may not be as simple as it seems. High school students are living in the moment, and while they may have plans for the future, working on those plans today is not a top priority. For a teen who has a test to study for, a new video game to master, a friend in crisis, or a chat she's in the middle of, *now* is just not the right time.

Andrea had been asking her son for weeks to come up with a list of colleges that interested him. Each time she tried to start the conversation, her son said he had something he needed to do. Finally, she told him she would no longer bring up the subject of college on weeknights when he had homework and other priorities. Instead she asked him to meet with her for an hour each

Sunday afternoon for the next month so that they could organize the college application process. By scheduling an appointment and setting a time limit of one hour, she helped overcome her son's feelings of being overwhelmed by "all this college talk."

On that first Sunday afternoon, Andrea asked her son to make a list of any schools he had been considering. Then she asked him to go online during the coming week and read through the application process for two of those schools. They looked at a calendar to think about when they could visit some campuses. With Sunday afternoons established as "college planning time," the two fell into a routine that made the search much more comfortable and productive.

THE CAMPUS TOUR

Every school is selling students (and their parents) on the unique opportunities they offer. Any campus tour will be a well-scripted promotion showcasing the newest high-tech classrooms, the most stunning architectural features, the best dorm rooms, and face time with the most captivating professors. Cheerful tour guides will talk about the vast range of student activities; study abroad programs in world capitals; and internships in the dynamic business community just a short bus ride away. There may be promises of all-you-can-eat-all-day dining; personal trainers, tanning beds, and water slides in the recreation center; weekend trips to nearby winter resorts; and discounted student tickets for theater productions, concerts, and professional sports events. Families may walk away from a college visit thinking, "This sounds like a luxury cruise, not a college campus."

All these amenities can make a difference in the student experience, and it's hard for students to ignore them. They can also affect the cost of a college education, though. As you and your student visit campuses, it's helpful to take notes, snap photos, and consider those features that seem most important to a good education, as well as those that particularly resonate with your student.

Either before or after the official tour, take time to walk the campus on your own. Stop in the student union or wander into areas you may not have seen on the official tour, and watch the students. Are they talking about classes? Studying? Hurrying to the parking lot? Or are they glued to their electronics?

If you see people who look like staff or faculty, what are they doing? What are they talking about? Do they smile and say hello? Are they talking to—or ignoring—students? It's not wise to rush to judgment based on one person's attitude, but look for a collective impression.

One father noted, "We happened to see our tour guide an hour after we left the admissions office. She didn't see us, but she and another guide were talking together, and they both seemed so happy and confident. They weren't paid to be smiling then, so we figured our guide really meant everything she had said on our tour."

Also pay attention to how safe you and your student feel on campus. If you're in the area overnight, walk the grounds after sunset. Is the campus well lit? Are students out and about? Does it *feel* safe?

During the paring-down process, you can talk with your student about the overall atmosphere of the campuses you visited, as well as which of those extras are really important, and which schools provide all or most of the "must-haves." Some points to talk about with your son or daughter—and take note of—after a campus visit:

• What surprised or impressed your student the most? How would these highlights affect your student's life on campus?

- Were there things that your student didn't like? Would these impact your student's life on campus?
- What stands out as important? Does your student want to continue her high school band skills by playing in pep band? Work on a research project with a professor? Volunteer at a campus television station? Does the school offer the opportunities your student most wants?
- If your child is not yet sure which of several majors might be the right choice, are all the options available at the school?

The most important questions after a campus visit and during the decision process are, "How did it feel to be on that campus? Is it a place you want to be? Can you see yourself there?"

Although some of the perks on a college tour may seem too good to pass up, it's important to consider whether they will actually fit into your child's educational plan. Studying abroad might sound wonderful, but if your daughter is a student athlete, can she fit a semester abroad into her competition schedule? Does the closely regimented coursework of a nursing program leave time for the sculpture class that looks so interesting?

It's not uncommon for the first college visit to be a bust. Most teenagers don't like being out of their comfort zone, and a campus tour can feel like an entirely new experience. Students don't know what to look for or what questions to ask. They can feel pressured by overly exuberant tour guides, and the only thing they have to compare this college to is their high school. They might come home from a tour with more reasons to be skeptical than enthusiastic. There is some logic in scheduling that first visit at a school the student doesn't really want to attend, or you could arrange for a repeat visit to the first college after touring other campuses.

WEIGHING THE OPTIONS

There truly is a college for everyone—at least for everyone who completes high school or passes the General Education Diploma test (GED or High School Equivalency test). So, how do students decide?

While designations like "public/private" and "two-year/four-year" help categorize colleges and universities, there are small, midsize, and large colleges in both the public and private sectors. Public colleges usually have lower tuition costs than private schools, although scholarship and grant funds can help level the financial playing field, depending on a student's qualifications and a family's financial need. As a general rule, private colleges tend to be smaller and may offer more instructor face time, but fewer majors. Class sizes in public universities may be larger. Just about every school will have some great professors along with some who are not so great.

With the ever-growing cost of a college education, more and more students are starting out at community colleges as a way to reduce expenses. Tuition at a nearby public community college is almost always going to be less than at a four-year school, and by living at home instead of on campus, students save on room and board. They can still get their bachelor's degree from a popular state university or an esteemed private college by transferring for the last two years of school, and they can still qualify for good jobs and for graduate school.

It's not the college that students choose that makes a difference. It's how they approach their education. Whether students live at home or on campus, they can either attend class regularly or skip routinely. At both two- and four-year schools, students have the choice to do their homework faithfully, form study groups with classmates, seek out instructors as mentors, and get involved on campus. Research consistently shows that when students are curious, engaged, and willing to ask for help, they are likely to stay in school, graduate, and go on to a successful career, no matter what type of college they attended.

THE ETHICS OF COLLEGE ADMISSIONS

Students set their sights high during the college search, and families can't help but hope that their child will gain admission to a prestigious university. As the pressure increases, the entire process begins to feel like a fierce competition with students contending for the best schools, and colleges bidding for the best students.

A growing criticism of college admissions is that the process inherently benefits students from upper-income families. Applicants from wealthy families are more likely to attend high schools with counselors dedicated solely to working with college-bound students. They have more extracurricular opportunities based on their parents' wealth and ability to pay the fees and buy the equipment. They receive test preparation for college entrance exams, and they can purchase the services of a professional consultant to guide them through the application process.

As the stakes grow for admission to top-choice schools, the temptation increases to overstate a student's qualifications or misrepresent accomplishments. Unfortunately, some parents have condoned their student's deceptions or even carried them out on behalf of their student, all in the name of giving their child the best in life. This is obviously wrong for multiple reasons, including the fact that it deprives other students of a fair chance of admission. It also sets students up for failure. Applicants who wouldn't have been admitted on their own merits are not likely to succeed at a competitive college. In addition, if false information about their qualifications is discovered after they're admitted, these students face not only bad publicity and embarrassment but also the possibility of expulsion and loss of any credits earned.

Admissions offices rely on the integrity of applicants, and they trust that the application they receive is accurate and is the work of the student, not a parent or a paid consultant. In an effort to define an appropriate role for parents in the admissions process, the Harvard Graduate School of Education has developed guidelines for "Ethical Parenting in the College Admissions Process."[1] Among the recommendations:

Put the focus on your teen. Separate your own hopes from your student's. Know that the college your student attends is not a measure of your success as a parent. Check with your student frequently on how they want you involved in the college choice process.

Keep ethics in mind. As a parent, you are a role model for your children's character and for their moral and ethical choices now and in the future. Don't condone misrepresentation of accomplishments on applications or essays or participate in dishonesty in the admissions process.

Use the admissions process to teach ethics and empathy. Talk to your student about the inequity of access to higher education, from the application process to the cost of college. Ask your child to consider how to present their accomplishments truthfully, while telling their story compellingly.

THE PARENT PERSPECTIVE

The parent role in the college selection process is to guide, not to control. The hope is that parents can help students think about

---

1. R. Weissbourd, *Turning the Tide II: How Parents and High Schools Can Cultivate Ethical Character and Reduce Distress in the College Admissions Process*, Harvard Graduate School of Education, 2019.

factors they might not otherwise consider. For example, a life-long soccer player might refuse to look at any college that doesn't offer him a position on a varsity team. His parents may prompt him to think about intramural teams that offer opportunities to play. The future physician who doesn't see "pre-medicine" listed among the school's undergraduate majors might need to hear about the biology, chemistry, management, or psychology programs that offer a good background for medical school.

Parents also can be the gatekeepers in some of the areas that students don't think about and colleges rarely discuss. If your son or daughter has a mental or physical health condition that requires special accommodations, parents can make sure that their child receives information from the school about appropriate services.

Braden, a student with Asperger's syndrome, had applied at the two-year college near home and at the state university an hour away. His mother was convinced he would be better off living at home rather than in a dorm, so that he could maintain the routines that she knew worked well for him. She was confident he could handle the academics of college, but she worried about his social skills, time management, and how he responded to stressful situations. Braden's best friends were both going to the state university, though, and he wanted to go with them.

"We'll get a dorm room together. They know me. They know who I am. We'll be fine," he said.

The family called both schools for campus tours, and they asked for time with disability counselors while they were there. Each of the schools explained how they worked with students on the autism spectrum. The four-year school introduced Braden to two students who were part of an autism support group. With the presence of Braden's friends, who had known him since first grade, a weekly check-in schedule with the disability office, and the support of the student group, Braden's mother was willing to leave the final decision to her son.

"Worst-case scenario," she said, "we can get there in an hour if he needs to come home for a while."

In addition to addressing mental and physical conditions, parents help when they talk with their student about identity and social factors that typically are not addressed during campus tours. These include race/ethnicity, gender identity, sexual orientation, and other personal characteristics. A high school junior or senior probably is not thinking about how it could feel to be the only student of color on her floor in the residence hall. A seventeen-year-old who has recently come out as gay is usually not yet prepared to consider how a roommate might respond to his identity. Parents are more likely than their students to have these concerns in mind.

Admissions programs tend to focus on general information that applies to all students. Any mention of services and support for diverse students is usually brief, with an invitation to call for more information. It's important to listen for those details and take note of the offices and campus groups that can provide the support your student needs.

Increasingly, diversity information sessions are offered at a separate time for multicultural and lesbian, gay, bisexual, and transgender (LGBT) students and their families. These might be an evening or weekend program during the college application process or a presentation connected to the school's orientation program.

When Godfrey and Neema received an invitation for a multicultural session following the family orientation program at their daughter's school, they wondered whether they really needed to stay for an extra two hours at the end of the daylong orientation. They were both college graduates, and they felt like they had a good idea of what their daughter's experience would be on campus. Did they really have to attend another presentation?

Neema called the orientation office to ask what additional information the multicultural session would offer. As she expected, information would be presented about multicultural services and student groups. The program would include dinner, when a panel of current students would talk candidly about their positive and not-so-positive experiences on campus. "We'll also have people from most of our student services offices on hand. After orientation, parents usually have some questions they hadn't thought of before, and this is a good chance to get the answers. Plus you can identify people you might want to talk to later." The top selling point was that their daughter would be matched with a mentor—a faculty or staff member who would meet with her several times during the first year. "Parents tend to refer their students to the mentors if they hear that the student is struggling with something," the director said.

Although not all schools provide mentors for multicultural and LGBT students, these additional information sessions provide a valuable opportunity for parents to ask questions and meet staff who can provide guidance if unexpected challenges come up.

Families that live abroad and send their children to U.S. colleges also tend to foresee problems their students don't consider. Lilli had attended English-speaking schools abroad all her life while her father worked in Hong Kong, Tokyo, and Singapore, but she always expected to attend college in the United States. She considered herself a New Yorker and an American, since she spent a month every summer at her grandparents' apartment in Brooklyn, and she was sold on the idea of attending a small, private college in upstate New York. She was annoyed, though, when her parents cautioned her that there was no "international community" in that college town. They urged her to think about how isolated she could feel and asked her to at least visit some other schools with a reputation for attracting international students.

"What are you talking about?" she asked. "I won't be lonely. It's not like there are any language problems. From what I can tell, all freshmen are pretty much in the same boat when they start out. And if I do get lonely, I can always take a train to stay with Grandma and Grandpa for a weekend. I'll be fine."

"Third-culture kids," those who are citizens of one country but are raised in and adapt to life in another, can find it hard to adjust to a college that doesn't have a strong international flavor. They frequently don't know—or don't appreciate—the norms, music, or popular culture of their classmates. They often have more knowledge of international news and events and can be put off by the lack of interest their American classmates seem to have in global issues.

When Lilli and her parents were touring her first-choice campus and walked to the business district for their fourth meal in two days in the small town, she began to see her parents might have a point. Looking at the menu, she struggled to find anything that appealed to her.

"Hamburgers, french fries, clam chowder, tuna sandwich?" she said. "I would love a bowl of noodles and vegetables. Just some rice! I don't know that I want to admit you're right about me being lonely here, but I sure could get hungry."

THE RELUCTANT APPLICANT

While every parent imagines the college search will be the basis of rich discussions and enjoyable family trips, for many teens, parental guidance on a college tour is the last thing they want. All summer before his senior year, Noah refused any invitations to visit colleges and universities, protesting that the college he would go to was his choice, and he didn't need his parents' input. As he began school in the fall with no plans in mind, his father became insistent.

"You're going to have to figure this out in the next few months. You have to start looking at some colleges."

Still, Noah resisted. "I've got time! I don't know for sure what I want to study, so I have to figure that out first. Besides, some of my friends have been visiting schools for a year already, and it hasn't done any good. They still don't know where they want to go."

By October, his parents were feeling much more panicky than Noah was, but they knew their anxiety wasn't helping. Remembering the saying, "Sometimes help is not helpful," they offered to step back if Noah would take some initiative. They offered to give him the car keys and a full tank of gas if he would visit one school within a two-hour drive from home.

"It's your choice and your day. You don't need to commit to any school yet. We'd just like you to visit *one* so you have an idea of what the college search is all about."

For Noah, a road trip by himself was what he needed in order to take that first step. Other students who are reluctant to tour a campus with Mom and Dad might be willing to tag along with a friend's family on a college tour. They may be happier to go with an older brother or sister, or a favorite aunt or uncle. Although Noah didn't end up attending that first college, the visit gave him the incentive to start looking at additional choices.

COLLEGE: IT'S NOT FOR EVERYONE

The popular message is that life after high school has a well-established next step: four years of college. The truth, though, is that college is not the next, best step for all high school graduates. At least not yet. Some students are motivated to get a full-time job and start earning their own income. Others have no idea what to study or are not ready to make the kind of commitment that college requires. If that sounds like your son or daughter, the best course of action is to help your child think about what comes next, if not college. You shouldn't insist on a college education if your student doesn't want to go or is not ready.

Many colleges and universities will defer enrollment if a student applies but later decides to wait for a semester or a year before starting college. Some schools will offer to defer enrollment for a semester if a student's high school transcript doesn't quite meet admission standards.

A gap year might mean living at home and working, traveling, or participating in a volunteer program. These experiences usually help students identify interests or decide on a major. While they're exploring their options or working, they often figure out what they *don't* want to do for the rest of their life. Most young adults report that the experiences they gathered during a gap year gave them the motivation to get a good education. If a year off helps a student focus and develop a desire to go on to college, it's time well spent.

An online search for gap year programs provides links to numerous opportunities. High school counselors also should have some insights into what has worked for other students.

DO THE MATH

Financing a college education is a major investment that affects the whole family—now and for years into the future. Every family's financial situation is different, and if there are budgetary limitations, students need to understand those restrictions from the start. While parents shouldn't automatically rule out a high-tuition, private college—students may qualify for a financial aid package that makes the school affordable—they should let their son or daughter know if attending certain schools depends on a generous scholarship offer. Nothing is harder than to go through the whole college search, sorting through the options to make a final choice, only to hear, "We can't possibly afford that much." When the danger is risking parents' retirement funds or setting students up with loans they will struggle to repay, the kindest thing you can do is establish realistic financial limits and help your student focus the college search within those parameters.

How you pay for a college education depends on family circumstances. There is no one-size-fits-all advice. Each college and university has different resources for providing grants and scholarships, and almost every state has its own educational savings plans. Many families have saved for years for their children's college fund. Some earn enough in their annual income to send their children to any school that accepts them. Other students, because of their family's modest income, may receive generous grants. Middle-class families can be the most likely to struggle to pay the full price for college expenses. This is a time to consult a financial adviser or do your own careful research on how you can best contribute to your child's education.

The one consistent recommendation for all families is to fill out the Free Application for Federal Student Aid (FAFSA) form each year (https://studentaid.ed.gov/sa/fafsa), even if you don't believe your student will qualify. The majority of U.S. students are eligible for at least some financial aid. And families that are initially declared ineligible may later find their circumstances changed by the loss of a job or incapacity of a wage-earner. If that happens, the school's financial aid office may be able to reconsider your student's aid package; it will help to have the FAFSA information on file.

After a student is accepted at a college or university, the school will use the FAFSA report to determine a financial aid package. The package will include any federal, state, or institutional scholarships and grants the student qualifies for. It also defines the student's and parents' expected contributions. It may include work-study funds, a federal student aid program that supports part-time work for students who qualify.

The arrival of the financial aid package might be a family's first notice of what college will actually cost for *their* student, at *this* particular school. Up to this point, any numbers have been rough estimates. Some families will suffer sticker shock.

"We've been saving for years, and we thought we could afford college!" one father protested. "When we went to the college fair, every private college said they offered scholarships and grants, and their school would end up costing about the same as a public university. Now it looks like we'll have to borrow money, and my son is going to graduate with debt."

While students can appeal their offer and ask for more financial aid, the answer is likely to be "No." Schools make the best awards they can up front, based on the student's academic and personal profile, taking into account the composition and the financial need of the entire pool of applicants.

When comparing financial aid packages from different institutions, you may want to create your own comparison chart. The school with the highest amount in grants and scholarships is not always the best deal. Make sure you're considering all expenses from each school. Terminology differs, but the bottom line will show how much your student is expected to pay and what the family contribution will need to be. Keep in mind that there can be extras not included in the package, such as the cost to travel home multiple times each year from a distant state or any expenses your student requires beyond the typical college costs.

A generous scholarship offer is tempting, but look carefully at the details. Is it a one-time, one-year scholarship that will not be available all four years? If the student is expected to maintain a minimum grade point average, is that realistic? A freshman's first semester is stressful, and it's not unusual for students to earn a full grade point below their high school average. If students decide to change their major, is the scholarship still valid? Find out if additional scholarships might be available in future years and how students qualify for those. If no work-study funds are listed, is there still a chance to work at an on-campus job?

NARROWING THE OPTIONS

The stress of choosing a college grows as the senior year progresses. Students become anxious as they see their friends begin to receive offers of acceptance. By mid-January, when the first application deadlines for colleges have passed and when the highest-achieving students have started to confirm their admissions, the apprehension can feel oppressive. "What's wrong with me? No one wants me."

When their own acceptance letters finally arrive, thick packets from multiple colleges, the emotions become more complex.

"Four schools accepted me! So now I have to turn some of *them* down?"

Students often will vacillate between wanting parents' input and wanting no conversation at all about college. Ryan's parents struggled to offer the right amount of input while assuring their son that the choice was his.

"You should make the decision you think is best for you," they said.

For Ryan, their trust in his decision only added to the pressure. "There are all these things to consider. Cost, location, majors, the kind of students who go there, whether I'll be happy there for four years. I know I'm supposed to figure it out and make a decision. My parents say they'll support whatever I choose, but no one ever told me how to make a decision this important. How do I know I'll get this right?"

Although families might make charts and spreadsheets with all the pros and cons of each college under consideration, ultimately the choice comes down to which school simply feels right.

"I KNOW WHAT I WANT"

Students might choose a college because of its national ranking or because they could do ocean research there. But more often the final decision is based on a visceral reaction. One applicant sat outdoors alone for an hour watching the students on a campus he was considering. When he met up with his mother, he declared, "I can *rule* this place!"

A student picked a college in Atlanta because she liked the furniture in the student union. She could see herself studying there. Another young woman turned down a generous scholarship offer because the students she met during an overnight stay on campus seemed to be focused "only on clothes and parties."

Students make their college choice because they fall in love with the library's view of the ocean, they can't resist the sunlight on an Arizona mountainside, or the campus architecture reminds them of Harry Potter books. In every case they feel, "I just want to be *here*."

One student told her mother, "I want a school that's bigger than me—a place I won't outgrow in four years, and I know this is it."

When students are finally sure of their decision, it's important for parents to honor that choice—if they can. But if it means years of debt or financial worries that linger for a decade or more, be assured that students can succeed with an education from an affordable school.

In those cases where the family simply cannot afford the school the student has chosen, or if parents are convinced the school is genuinely not a good fit, the next step is for parents to calmly and explicitly explain their reasoning, listen to and empathize with their student's perspective, and resume the search for a mutually acceptable option. Too many times, when parents "lay down the law" and make the choice for their son or daughter, the student begins college with a poor attitude and ultimately finds a way to prove to her parents that they were wrong.

On the other hand, when students are excited about their college and arrive on campus with a positive attitude, they are more likely to adjust well. That lays the groundwork for the entire college experience.

REJECTED? NOW WHAT?

Even as students prioritize their dream schools and their safety schools during the admissions process, they will be gravely discouraged by the letter that says, "Thank you for applying. We had many excellent applicants, and we regret to inform you . . ."

For many students, this is the first time in their lives they've been rejected. They've been brought up in a world where they were told they could do or be anything they wanted. Even when they haven't excelled, they've been praised and rewarded for every minor achievement, or just for *trying*. They have the trophies and certificates declaring them an all-American scholar, a dedicated athlete, or a clean-cabin camper. When they applied for colleges, they imagined they actually would get into that highly competitive school.

Parents are equally surprised and dismayed when their student's application is denied. They have eighteen years of evidence in scrapbooks, and plenty of photos and videos on their phones, proving that their child is outstanding. It's jarring to think someone is saying he's "not quite good enough." Most college admissions officers have been accused of "ruining my kid's life." They've also heard the pleas, "It's just one more student. You have ten thousand students. It's not like every seat in every class is going to be full every day."

It's at least as devastating to be placed on a waitlist and told, "Your application demonstrated great promise, and we have put you on our waitlist. We will let you know your status after May 15. In the meantime, we encourage you to secure a place at another college."

If a student has been placed on the waitlist, and some compelling new factors have come up since the application was sent in, it's worthwhile for a student to contact the admissions office with the information. Maybe he wrote a personal essay that was published in a national magazine, or he was awarded second place in the state History Day competition. But that waitlist advice is right—students should secure a place in the class of a school that wants them. It may be the first rejection in a child's life, but it won't be the last.

RESILIENCE AND GRIT

To an applicant, hearing that a college has turned her down might feel like the worst thing that can happen. It's not. This can be one of those teachable moments—opening your student's eyes to possibilities she hasn't yet considered.

In recent years, professors and higher education administrators have complained that students lack the resilience and grit they need to deal with the challenges of college and life in general. College students obsess over receiving what they think is a poor grade—a B or C—when they're accustomed to getting only A's. They're deeply offended by a roommate who doesn't respect their request to turn down the music or empty a wastebasket.

They can't handle being denied access to a class they wanted to take. Meanwhile, more significant failures, disappointments, breakups, or life events cause stress and anxiety that result in a crush of calls to college counseling offices.

Merriam-Webster defines resilience as "an ability to recover from or adjust easily to misfortune or change." Grit is described as "unyielding courage in the face of hardship or danger." Parents frequently get the blame for creating "snowflake kids" with their "snowplow parenting." And while protecting their children is a family's most basic responsibility, parents also are responsible for teaching their children to cope with disappointments and rebound from failures.

Research shows that children and young adults build resilience and develop grit through positive relationships with parents or other adults who support and believe in them.[2] A parent's job is not to prevent every failure or fix every problem for their child. The goal is to help children recognize that life includes challenges, changes, and failures that give them the experiences they need for building a solid path to success. There is a sense of achievement, along with valuable life lessons, that come from solving problems and learning how to avoid making the same mistakes again.

Hopefully, by the time they're seniors in high school, teens will have some experience with handling failure and know what they can do to rebound—go for a run or a swim, call a friend, spend time outdoors, or listen to music. When they're ready to tackle the problem again, family members help by slowing down instant reactions and reframing the situation.

When Cara learned she hadn't passed the performance audi-

---

2. A. G. Waithaka, T. M. Furniss, and P. N. Gitimu, "College student mindset: Does student-parental relationship influence the student's mind-set?" *Research in Higher Education Journal* (June 2017): 32.

tion for the fine arts program at her top choice school, she was devastated.

"There's nowhere else I want to go," she complained. "Mom, I *have* to get into this program! It's everything I ever wanted! How can I tell my voice teacher I didn't make it? She said I could be a professional, but now I'm a certified failure."

"You're not a failure," her mother reassured her. "That school has a really competitive program. It doesn't mean your music career is done. Maybe it means looking at different programs or different ways of studying music. You have the Civic Chorale rehearsal Saturday. Is there someone in the chorale you might be able to talk to? Just ask a couple of people for ideas?"

After conversations with one of the chorale members, her high school counselor, and her voice teacher, Cara decided to confirm her acceptance at her second-choice school. Two years later, she was studying for a degree in music therapy.

"I've got a professor this semester who does research on how music can help people with dementia," she told her mother. "I'm looking at jobs in music therapy—maybe at a hospital or senior care center. I feel like this is a job I could do that would be *important*."

Dealing with rejection is something like dealing with grief. There are stages to go through and time is an important part of the process. Students are likely to react first with denial, believing this must all be a mistake. They will be angry. They'll want to bargain with the admissions office. They'll feel terrible for a while. Eventually they'll be in a place emotionally where they can consider other options.

Students are justified in feeling bad about a rejection. Parents also have a right to feel disappointment, but too often part of a student's suffering is feeling that they've let their parents down. It doesn't help your child to know you made an angry phone call to the admissions counselor or demanded special favors.

Parents can be most helpful by acknowledging their children's feelings and allowing some time for them to take it in. The next step is encouraging them to start thinking about alternative plans and learn from this experience. Since Plan A is not going to work, what are the options?

As James Yorke, University of Maryland professor and expert on chaos theory, says, "The most successful people are those who are good at Plan B." One simple change of direction can lead to a far better outcome. Millions of college applicants have been rejected from their first-choice schools. The resilient ones have gone on to other colleges, found them to be a great fit, and proceeded to make the best friends of their lives. They have become successful students, and they have gone on to rewarding careers. Being open to that single change of direction didn't end anything; it led to a better dream.

MAY 1: IS THAT YOUR FINAL DECISION?

Some students commit to a college as soon as they get their first letter of acceptance. Others won't even apply until high school graduation is over. But for those students who are weighing multiple acceptance offers, May 1 is College Decision Day.

Confirming their acceptance, however, is not the last decision students will be making. It really just begins the flow of communication that calls for choices about any number of things. From your student's standpoint, this is personal. These decisions will affect the most basic aspects of college life: Will he live in a single room, a double, or a suite? How many meals each week will he eat in the dining center? Should he move into a freshman hall, live on the Spanish-language floor, or request apartment-style housing with upper-classman students?

Parents worry that these decisions will affect the student's well-being and the family finances, in some cases for years to come. As a parent, you might see some pitfalls in selecting a freshman dorm or in choosing a hall with no quiet hours, and you want to help your child avoid the potential problems. Parents feel more urgency about meeting deadlines and more caution about answering questions completely and thoroughly.

When Jeremy filled out his housing application, he didn't think twice about what kind of a room he wanted. He wanted a single. He had always had his own bedroom, and it didn't occur to him to consider any other choice. After filling in all his information, he asked his mother for her credit card to pay the deposit fee. He was a little offended when she said she wanted to see what she was paying for. The first thing she noticed was that his single-room selection would cost considerably more than a double. A triple or a four-person suite would be even more economical.

"Jeremy, you marked down that you want a single room. You didn't even talk to me about this. I think you should consider one of these less expensive rooms."

Jeremy had plenty of reasons why he should have a single. He would study better if he was by himself, he said. He needed quiet to concentrate on homework. What if his roommate wanted to play loud music all the time? What if the roommate had friends over when Jeremy needed to study or sleep?

Slowly it became obvious that both Jeremy and his mother had other concerns they weren't talking about. In addition to the financial impact of the decision, Jeremy's mother was worried that her son might not make friends. He had never been particularly outgoing, and his best friends from high school were going to different colleges. She was afraid that it would be more difficult for him to meet people if he lived in a single.

Jeremy had never mentioned it to his mother, but on an overnight band trip a few months earlier, he was teased unmercifully about his snoring. He didn't want roommates complaining all year that his snoring was keeping them awake.

Jeremy and his mother both agreed that there were complications to this seemingly simple decision. They set the application form aside for a few days and agreed to give it some more thought. Jeremy's mother made a call to the nurse at their clinic, who suggested that nasal strips from the drugstore could reduce the snoring. In a moment of enlightenment, Jeremy realized that in a four-person suite with two bedrooms, he would have good odds of being matched with at least one other snorer. And as it turned out, his suite mate was a sound sleeper who almost always went to bed earlier than Jeremy. There were never any complaints about snoring.

Not all decisions end quite as well, though. Many students, caught up with the closing events of high school, set their messages aside and plan to deal with them later. As the days go by, important responses are forgotten, and parents don't know deadlines are being missed.

One afternoon, Andy's coworker mentioned that his daughter had taken math and language tests online to determine what course levels she would be taking in the fall. Andy's son, Troy, was going to the same college, but he hadn't said anything about placement tests. That evening Andy asked Troy if he had taken any tests for college.

"No, not yet," Troy said. "I'm pretty sure I have something about that in my email, though." Andy went with him to look for the schedule and discovered a long list of unopened emails from the college.

"What is all this? I didn't even know you were *getting* these things—here's a notice about your financial aid, something about orientation, testing dates. Have you responded to any of these?" Andy asked.

When students apply to or are accepted at a college, they receive a campus email account and password. Because federal law recognizes college students as adults, the information goes to the student, no matter who will be paying the bills. Parents don't always see what arrives, and the only way you will know what needs to be done is if your student tells you. Parents may think this makes no sense, but from a developmental perspective, students need to start assuming responsibility.

Certainly, you want to be kept up to date on the choices your student is making, and it's not unusual for parents to end up supervising the decisions. Some parents ask for their student's passwords or PIN numbers; some even select the passwords for their child.

When students give away their password to a family member, they are learning that "it's okay to share passwords with the people who love you." Too often, that translates into giving passwords to best friends, boyfriends or girlfriends, or roommates. There are many examples of students signing up an ex-girlfriend on a pornography website, an angry roommate dropping a student out of all her classes, or a former best friend using a student's credit card information to place online orders.

Parents make a strong impact if they tell their child that no one, not even Mom and Dad, should have their passwords or PIN numbers. If there are payments you need to make, or if there is a concern that at some point you will need to access your student's accounts, establish expectations about when, why, and how you will obtain that information.

Most colleges have a process for parents to access the information they need for paying bills. That process starts with the student signing a release giving parents permission to see those records. If you're concerned about a possible emergency where you will need certain information, you can keep a sealed envelope with passwords in a safe place. What's important is that the student understands the importance of safeguarding personal information.

For Andy's son, the placement test situation was not as hopeless as it had seemed. By calling the college, Troy received an access code to take his placement tests late—but he needed to learn some organizational skills. He had an idea of what information had arrived. He just needed a system for managing it all. In a single evening, Andy helped him sort through the unopened messages, printing off the important ones and using a highlighter to mark dates and a calendar to note deadlines.

All the notices that are pouring in can seem daunting to a prospective freshman. Every communication is asking for some kind of decision or action step. Some of those decisions seem simple, but students might not know if it makes sense to order season football tickets, sign up for student organizations, or buy a bus pass for the local transit system. Students want to make the choices themselves, but they're paralyzed by the fear of making mistakes.

This is your chance to provide guidance while empowering your student to make independent decisions. Let your child know that you're willing to talk about the options, but give her authority to make her own decisions. Let her know if you want a voice on issues that affect finances. Tell her she may eventually wish she had chosen differently on some of those decisions, but that doesn't mean she made a mistake. We all make choices based on the information we have available to us at the time.

QUICK TIPS FOR STUDENTS

- Filling out college applications may not be your top priority on any given day, but a few months after high school graduation, you will want to be starting your new life. Selecting a college takes time and work; it's easier if you do a little every week. What can you do *this week* to move the process forward?

- The college choice is yours to make, but it affects your family, too. Talk to your family about any limits on the cost of college and any limits on how far away from home you can go. Also be willing to explain your reasons for applying to the schools you've chosen.

- If you have a dream school, it can be hard to imagine any other choice, and it's discouraging to think you might not get in. Go ahead and apply to that college, but after you send in the application, take a look at other options. Someplace else might end up being even better.

- Finish high school strong! When you start college, you will need the information they were giving you during your senior year.

- Review college information as it arrives, figure out what kind of response is needed, and be sure to reply before the deadline.

- Tell your parents about any decisions that will have a financial impact. If you're asking your parents to pay for any unexpected expenses, give them your reason for needing to incur the extra cost. If they can't add any more to their budget, figure out if you can fund the expense yourself.

CHAPTER 2

A Summer of Change

Making the Most of the Months Before College

Each year as a new group of high school graduates and their parents watch the calendar pages turn toward August, emotions begin to churn. Mothers and fathers who were so relieved and proud when the college acceptance notices arrived a few months ago find themselves wondering, "How is this kid going to make it at college? Just this week, he's managed to lose his sunglasses, a bike lock, and a pair of shoes."

Students who are confident in their college choice one day are convinced a day later that they will never fit in. "I think the school made a mistake when they accepted me. I was probably the last person they picked, and I'm going to be the stupidest freshman on campus. I don't even have the right clothes. No one will like me. It's just not going to work."

For these students and their families, the issue is simple: Everything is changing. The excitement and anticipation that peaked in late spring turns to rebellion during the "senior summer." Recent graduates are rejecting curfews and failing to show up for family meals, defending their freedom by pointing out, "In a couple of months you won't *ever* know what I'm doing."

Meanwhile, parents are struggling to maintain peace in the family. Bickering among brothers and sisters reaches new heights.

One parent or the other is locked in conflict with their future collegian. Parents listen to their child's unending complaints about the community or the small-mindedness of the neighbors, and they begin to long for the day when they can finally take this miserable, unhappy kid to college. A minute later, they can't bear to think of her leaving. "I'm going to miss her so much!"

What's a parent to do? Advice flows in from every direction, but each suggestion conflicts with at least one other.

"Give them space." *"Be sure to set clear boundaries."*

"Make sure you've talked about the critical issues." *"You can't review a lifetime of lessons in one short summer."*

"Reassure them that you'll miss them." *"Don't lay a guilt trip on them about leaving."*

The whole family has been planning for college for years, but now parents can't help but wonder what this will all mean. When changes are pending, emotional flare-ups are a natural reaction. The challenges are to identify the real issues as they occur and to recognize what each member of the family is feeling.

LIFE SMARTS: THE REAL MEASURES OF COLLEGE SUCCESS

As comforting as it was to finally firm up the college decision, at least some of the emotions that students and parents face during the senior summer might be tied to buyer's remorse. Parents ask themselves, "What have we done? How can we afford this?" Students wonder if they're ready for this next step. Suddenly, college seems *serious*. Teens feel like they're taking a giant leap to a much higher level—college! And they're not sure they're ready. What they don't yet realize is that it's not purely intellect that promises success in college. Life smarts make all the difference, and that practical knowledge that students have learned through a lifetime of experiences will get them through . . . if they use it.

College students should have the ability to excel, or at least get by, at any school that accepts them. Schools don't admit students who are not academically prepared for the rigor of their coursework. When students fail during college, it can almost always be traced back to problems outside the classroom. Students improve their chances of college success by taking over more of their own responsibilities before leaving home. When they prove to themselves that they can manage daily life, they gain confidence in their ability to take care of themselves.

The most common reason for college failure is that students have not learned to think about how they use their time. Parents—especially mothers—have been directing the family schedule for years, for very good reasons. They need to coordinate everyone's calendar. They know the annual Scouting banquet is on Wednesday, and their student has a chemistry test Thursday, so they remind him to study for the exam on Tuesday night. They want to avoid arguments about the bathroom in the morning, so they wake their children at different times and set limits on time in front of the mirror. Consequently, students arrive at college with little experience in managing their own schedules.

Before college begins, have your student take over more of those scheduling responsibilities. Explain why time management is important to a college student. If your daughter is late for work or an appointment because she didn't get up on time, let her deal with the consequences. It's much better to face the outcome of a mistake while living in the protective environment of home, or under the oversight of a teacher or supervisor who knows her well, than it will be when she's in college on her own.

Students also should begin managing their health care on their own. In most cases, when a child or teenager gets sick, parents take over. It's what parents are supposed to do. But before your student leaves for college, when anyone in the family gets sick—or if you hear about a friend who is sick—use the situation as a teachable moment. Talk about the fact that students *do* come down with a cold or the flu at some point. There's always the possibility of scrapes, bruises, or other injuries and illnesses. When that happens, what will your child do? How will he decide whether to call a doctor? Let your student start managing medical appointments now, keeping in mind that you may have to approve the appointment or go along if your child is under eighteen. See Chapter 9 for more suggestions on preparing your student for health care issues.

There are a number of other basic skills that first-year advisers and residence hall staff agree that all students should know before they arrive:

- *Balancing a bank account and managing debit and credit cards.* Ideally, students should have learned about checking accounts, debit cards, credit cards, and payment apps during high school. By the time college classes begin in the fall, they should understand the importance of recording withdrawals and deposits and the mechanics of reconciling a bank statement or monthly bill. They need to know about late payment penalties, interest charges, overdrafts, and annual fees. More information about finances can be found in Chapter 7.

- *Doing their laundry.* Yes, there are laundries that will wash, fold, and iron for students, but this is a skill that everyone should learn. This means, at minimum, emptying pockets; separating red, purple, and maroon clothing from light colors, and lights from dark; measuring laundry detergent; knowing what not to wash (notably, sport jackets, ties, anything labeled "dry clean only"); loading clothes loosely into the washing machine rather than stuffing a month's worth of laundry with bedsheets into a single load; sorting delicates for hand washing; keeping wool sweaters away from hot water and dryers; and removing clothes from washers and dryers soon after the machine stops.

- *Ironing a shirt, threading a needle, replacing a button, repairing a ripped seam.* Be pitiless about insisting your student take care of his or her wardrobe during the summer before college. Your child should know that a minor wardrobe malfunction can be fixed.

- *Preparing or obtaining basic food.* A missed meal means students must occasionally find food to get through the night. Residence hall staff are dismayed at the number of college-level students who are unable to read and comprehend the instructions on microwave meals—or to clean up the residue when food bubbles over and burns. Make sure your child has, at least once in his life, placed an order for food delivery, paid for it, and tipped the driver.

- *Trusting their instincts when they feel uneasy or unsafe.* Most parents remember to tell their daughter to avoid walking across campus alone at night; young men need the same message. No matter their gender, students also need to hear about date rape and acquaintance rape. Students enter into new friendships with trust and confidence, and they often ignore or downplay suggestive and threatening behaviors. More information on this topic is discussed in Chapter 8.

- *Making responsible decisions regarding alcohol, drugs, and sex.* The opportunity for partying will be greater at college than ever before. Remind your student of your expectations and encourage him or her to be careful and to take care of friends. Alcohol, drugs, and sex are discussed more fully in Chapter 8.

- *Knowing how to change a tire, where to go for an oil change, how to operate a car wash, if they will have a car on campus.* No student should spend more time worrying about or reacting to car problems than studying. If they do, they shouldn't have a car. They also should know what to do if there is an accident, and how to respond if they are stopped by the police.

"LAST TIME" SYNDROME

As you sit at the picnic table in the backyard on the Fourth of July, a wave of nostalgia washes over you. "She'll be leaving soon. This could be the last picnic we will ever have together." Wistful thoughts overcome you as you drive past your child's favorite restaurant, go to the mall together, watch a video on Sunday night, or bake his favorite dessert on a rainy Saturday afternoon.

Some parents try so hard to savor each moment that they end up in a constant state of sorrow. Others focus on every complaint their student makes and miss the good times. This last summer before college is a series of emotional peaks and valleys. Your feelings might be different if this is your first child, a middle child, or the last to leave home, but no matter what, there will be trying times.

At some colleges, new student orientation begins in June and sessions continue through mid-July. During the first weeks of orientation, parents are still planning the high school graduation party, and they're focused on the guest list and menu for the upcoming celebration. They might take notes about tasks that need to be done before school starts, but they are confident they have plenty of time.

Midway through orientation season, parents are exhausted from cleaning up after the party, and they're badgering their student to write thank-you notes. They have no problem with the idea that their student will be moving away from home in a few months—September is still too far away to take it seriously.

By July, though, parents are in tears when they realize that they're counting the time to move-in day in weeks, not months. "I promised myself I wouldn't cry. I'm just not ready for this!"

And it's not only the mothers who are affected by the transition. A father will gulp back the lump in his throat when he watches his daughter walk away with her orientation group. Each week parents' reactions become increasingly intense, sometimes going beyond sadness and tears to bursts of anger.

A family arrived for orientation one morning, and the daughter registered while her parents looked on. Then they all crossed the room to the check-in table where parents signed in for the family orientation program. When the father couldn't find name badges for himself and his wife, he began berating the student volunteer who was staffing the registration desk.

"We paid for this program a month ago! Where are our name tags? This is ridiculous! I want to talk to someone in charge. Now!"

The intensity of his reaction was a surprise to the volunteer as well as to his family. His daughter finally remembered that she had rescheduled her orientation date, but she forgot to change the registration for her parents. Their names were on the list for the next day. The volunteer quickly ordered name tags and updated their registration. After the problem was solved, the man's wife returned to the registration table to explain that this was their youngest child and their only daughter.

"Our sons went to a college just a few miles from home, so it didn't feel that far away. And my husband has always been protective of our daughter—he wanted her to stay closer to home. This is really hard for him."

In the last weeks before school begins, parents' patience wears thin as the rosy glow of the *image* of sending their student to college collides with the stark reality of saying good-bye. Anything about the school that seems less than perfect is cause for alarm. A week before move-in a mother wonders how capable the residence hall director is if he doesn't know how big the closet is.

"I have to buy storage bins that will fit in the closet. You don't have any measurements? You don't even know if there are shelves in the closet? Have you ever *been* in these rooms?"

The emotions you feel as school approaches are legitimate. Your real fear is that no one will be looking out for your child. You deserve rational explanations and full answers to your questions. But when you begin to fume, ask yourself if your frustration is with the school, your student, or the larger situation—your family is changing.

BUT I HAVE PLANS!

As the end of summer approaches, parents wonder if they have already lost their child. They try to schedule a family weekend before their son leaves for college, but he has something lined up for each date they suggest. They would like to take him shopping, but he's booked every evening for the next week and a half.

In the last weeks before school starts, students are not focusing on packing, cleaning their room, or being with family. They're spending all their time with high school classmates, making every effort to cement the friendships they're leaving behind. At this moment in your child's life, he has much more in common with his friends than he does with you.

The senior summer holds magical moments for soon-to-be college students. During the day, prospective freshmen may be working a full-time job, being treated like adults. Every evening, stretching long into the night, they're meeting up with friends, picturing all the possibilities their future holds. This is, for many students, the best social period of their lives so far, and while it's easy to imagine a great future in distant and exciting places, it's impossible to think that these friends will be connecting only through apps, texts, and emojis in just a few short weeks.

Leaving friends might include the end of a serious romance. Any student who is in a relationship during the summer before college is at least thinking about what will happen in the fall. There may be a mutual understanding that they'll date other people at college. There may be promises that "We'll always be together." Or there may be disagreements and long talks about what comes next. On the other hand, sometimes there is no discussion until a breakup phone call—or worse, a quiet change in relationship status on social media—a week after one of them leaves home.

Your suggestion that your student could take time away from friends in order to have dinner with you, go shopping, or pack a few boxes seems to an emerging adult like a pointless request. After all, you've always been there for your child, and she fully expects that you always will be.

Thinking about leaving home is both exciting and frightening for young adults, but they don't dare express their concerns about the upcoming changes. Instead they might just become angry or indignant. When you tell your son to move his sports gear out of the hallway, he's resentful that you're treating him like a kid; if you tell him to make his own decisions, he feels as though you're abandoning him. If you remind your daughter about packing, you're hounding her, but if you don't offer to find some boxes, you obviously aren't interested in helping.

The biggest problems seem to crop up between the student and whichever parent he or she most closely resembles. It's hard to imagine major confrontations as a compliment, but if you and your daughter are arguing constantly, and you're wondering how you could have become such an unbearable parent, it's probably a sign that she is much like you. And that disturbs her endlessly.

Younger brothers or sisters react to the fear of change as well. Preteens are troubled by the idea of their big brother or sister leaving home, and they become clingy and emotional. "Why do you have to go away? Won't you miss me? Who will be here when I come home from school?"

Siblings just a few years younger, those who are themselves starting to think about college, see great possibilities as they watch the freshman prepare to leave home. They're imagining their own transition to college, and in the meantime, they can see the personal potential in their sibling's departure. "Do I get to move into her bedroom now?" "If he's getting a new laptop, where's mine?"

Just when your soon-to-be college student feels like all the lights should be shining brightly on him, his little sister is demanding all the attention, it feels like Dad only wants him around to clean out the garage, and Mom is enthusiastically buying him laundry detergent and new underwear. To the departing child, this all adds up to a slowly festering suspicion that "everyone is a little too happy that I'm leaving."

LAST-MINUTE ADVICE

All across the country, as long July days give way to sweltering August nights, parents of college-bound students lie awake perspiring from dread as much as from the heat: "Did I talk to him about tracking his bank account online?" "What will she do if she gets sick?" "I don't think she understands how much trouble she can get into at college parties."

You have only a few short weeks to pass along all the advice you think your child will need. What if you forget something important?

High school graduates rarely listen patiently as their parents deliver sermons about being safe or earning good grades. There are things your student needs to know for the purely practical demands of coping with life at college, and there are things your student's school hopes you will discuss with your child. There are even a few things your child would appreciate hearing from you. The trick is to figure out when you're offering useful information as opposed to unwanted advice or a rulebook of warnings.

VIRTUAL FRIENDS

The first college "friends" that your son or daughter meets might just be the several hundred students who joined the school's social media group for incoming freshmen. Searching the site for anyone who shares an interest in ultimate Frisbee or who likes the same computer game could be the beginning of a close bond or even the meet-up point for a whole group of friends.

First-year students are both excited about and intimidated by the thought of leaving home and gaining independence. One of their first goals is to establish the social support—the friendships—they fear they're leaving behind. Certainly, they will stay in touch with their old friends from high school, summer camps, or sports. Social media, texting, and various apps give them the tools to quickly update their status for everyone to see. But they need to surround themselves with friends in their college environment—allies they can talk to, count on, and turn to as they start this new venture. At the same time, though, they're still in the process of figuring out who they want to become. Finding people like yourself isn't easy when you're not yet sure who you are.

If New Year's Day provides an incentive to commit to new resolutions, the start of college is an even greater opportunity for students to reinvent themselves. Social media offers an ideal stage to try out a new persona. Before Tamara joined her class's social network, she carefully crafted a profile to portray herself as the studious biology major she intended to become. She posted a photo showing herself standing waist-deep in a pond, wearing chest waders. She added a few lines about the volunteer work she was doing at a community park, identifying macroinvertebrates. It wasn't until months later that Tamara learned her roommate had taken an instant dislike to her, thinking she was facing a year of hearing about bugs and algae.

"Why didn't you at least mention that your summer job was teaching yoga? Or that you won first prize in your school's cupcake contest? I would have known right away I'd won the roommate lottery."

Students want to be liked. They post information to make themselves look interesting, friendly, or whatever their perception is of "collegiate." They imagine that their classmates are all outstandingly clever or have the most amazing lives, so they take a small piece of their own life and make it seem like the whole. As they progress through school, they'll become more comfortable with their multifaceted identities and present themselves more authentically. For now, though, they are defining themselves and judging others with incomplete information.

If your student looked at his own posts honestly, he might see that the image he projects does not really reflect his everyday life. Remind your student that people tend to share only their best selfies, their greatest successes, and the most important events in their lives. Students—and parents—who are checking roommates' profiles online are wise to withhold judgment until they get a more complete picture.

PACKING, PILING, OR PROCRASTINATING?

Some students start packing boxes for college in June. Some can't decide what they will need, so they make a giant pile of clothes, bedding, and belongings, adding and subtracting items for weeks on end. Others postpone even thinking about packing until the last minute. Based on student feedback, all of these methods work equally well. Every student forgets something; every student brings more than they need. Even the late starters who spend their last night at home throwing things into boxes end up with the basics.

As much fun as it can be to plan your student's decor, this is not the time to take charge of every detail. Rather than picking out an accent table and lamps for the dorm room, ask your student to contact roommates to compare what they each will bring. There's no point in duplicating large items.

By planning and setting up the room together, new roommates pick up useful clues about each other's personality, values, background, and financial resources. A shopping trip is often the students' first shared outing. What you can do to be helpful is encourage your student to use these room setup conversations as a way to get to know roommates, share ideas about decorating, and find ways to compromise.

Students do not have to bring everything they own. Hall directors advise, "We don't have space for horse trailers in the parking lot. If your possessions won't fit into a minivan or a large SUV, they probably won't fit into a residence hall room."

A family shopping trip is a college send-off tradition. Ask your student to make a list based on the school's suggested packing list or find an online list. Know that no one needs everything on the "ultimate college packing list." Anything you're doubtful about can be picked up at a campus-area store after your student moves in, and online shopping will provide items that become important later.

Most students don't want your help with the packing, but they will not complain if you offer to put together some specific items—a get-well kit in case they come down with a cold, a package of study rations to get them through the first couple of weeks, or a tool kit and connection cords for basic repairs and chargers.

Health Kit

Put together some first-aid basics: a box of tissues, a packet of bandages, antiseptic cream, cold and flu medication, and pain reliever. In addition, you can pack a "get-well kit" with instructions to open it in case of illness. In the kit, pack more of the essentials along with some extra items.

- Digital thermometer
- Throat lozenges
- Instant soup
- Tea bags
- Jar of honey
- Some of the comforts that worked when your child was small: a game, puzzle, graphic novel, coloring book and crayons, favorite video (most college students like to revert to childhood activities from time to time)
- A get-well card with a caring message, signed by family members

GOOD INTENTIONS, BAD RESULTS

Treating college as a new beginning, many students—with or without their doctor's advice—see this time as a chance to try life without the medication, therapy, or support groups that have long been part of their normal routine. The young woman with a learning disability is tired of being labeled, so she decides not to register with the college disability office. The athlete, who is sure that his structured training schedule means he no longer needs medication to help him concentrate, doesn't refill his prescription before leaving for school.

When absolutely everything in a student's life is changing, this is the worst possible time to give up the prescriptions and systems that have helped in the past.

In high school, Amy joined a support group led by the school psychologist. Her parents' divorce had been hard on her. The sessions were often emotionally draining, but the group helped her find answers to many of her questions and learn to cope with the questions that didn't have answers. By the time she left for college, she was two years beyond the crisis, and she was relieved at the thought of being done with group counseling.

A few weeks after Amy moved to campus, her mother became concerned about the tone of her daughter's phone calls. Amy sounded increasingly depressed and complained that "everything is so hard!" All she wanted was to come home.

Her mother suggested that she make an appointment with a counselor at the university, just to see if it might help. After a few appointments, Amy began to see how leaving home for college had resurrected some of her anxieties related to the divorce. She had never understood how her father could walk away from the family and start a new life; now she was doing the same thing. With a few more sessions, Amy found ways to make a fresh start for herself and still have plenty of room in her life for her mother.

It's understandable that students want a chance to give up those long-term treatments or medications. Parents, meanwhile, might support the idea that their child is ready to "move on." They hope that their son or daughter has overcome past problems, and college feels like the milestone that marks the cure. If the new challenges of college cause a recurrence of old illnesses or problems, though, parents are not there to monitor the signs. Students may be the last to detect their own regression, and when they need help the most, they could be incapable of looking for it.

College disability counselors understand that students want to try getting along without extra support. They will not force students with physical disabilities to use transportation services, and they won't insist that students with learning disabilities sign up for special accommodations if they don't want to. If the student eventually finds that extra assistance is needed, however, the disability office must have the paperwork and physician's reports documenting the health condition. Similarly, the student who falls into depression but has allowed his prescription to lapse will have to meet with a psychiatrist to obtain medication. Students are wise to file the forms before classes begin, even if they don't think they will ever need the assistance.

As challenging as it may feel for your student to talk about a mental or physical health condition, it can be important for a roommate or staff member to have that information. If your son's roommate doesn't recognize the compulsive or antisocial symptoms of Asperger's syndrome, he may conclude that your son is unfriendly or has taken offense for some reason. If he understands the symptoms, he can shrug it off or do some research to learn if what he's seeing is part of the condition. Similarly, a student who has learned to recognize the signs of an allergic reaction can call for help if her roommate cannot.

The Boy Scout motto, "Be Prepared," is the best advice parents can give. Your child can be assertive about demanding a fresh start, but having all the appropriate health records on hand is a simple insurance policy. A conversation between roommates is more likely to establish open understanding than create a barrier. If the time comes when you get a sense your child needs the support systems or medications that have helped in the past, you can encourage a visit to the disability office or a refill of a prescription.

COMMUTER CONCERNS

The transition to college is challenging even if it doesn't include a trip to Target for extra-long sheets or packing the car for Move-In Day on campus. Commuter students face their own set of adjustment issues and questions about their college choice. As high school friends are talking about leaving for college, commuters begin to rethink their decision to stay home.

Natalie had decided to enroll in a community college as a way to save money during her first two years. She just wished that the college wasn't quite so close. It was only three miles from home and within sight of her old high school. By the beginning of August, she was disappointed that she had passed up other opportunities, and she was envious of all her friends who were getting ready to leave town. When she thought about her first day of classes, only two things entered her mind: "Where am I supposed to park?" and "Who can I eat lunch with?"

She also had a nagging suspicion that college should somehow feel more important than it did. Her friends were comparing their residence hall assignments and talking about their new roommates. Their parents were all taking a couple of days off work to go with their children to orientation; her own parents merely left a note on the table the morning of Nat's welcome program: "Hope your day goes well! Looking forward to hearing about it tonight!"

That evening, after she had signed up for classes, she complained to her mother, "The only time they offer French is in the evening, and it's taught by Mrs. Jenkins from my high school. It's going to be just like last year."

For commuter students who attend a primarily residential school—a university where most of the freshmen live in dorms—the feeling of isolation can be even stronger. They go to orientation, and everyone is asking, "So, where are you from? What hall will you be living in?" The commuter is convinced that it's far more interesting to be the girl from Florida or the guy from Chicago than the kid from a few miles away.

All these emotions are expressed to parents not as frustration, but as disinterest. Commuter students often don't show much enthusiasm about college, and it's hard for parents to work up interest about the college experience when they see so little excitement from their child. The things parents do before school starts can make a great difference, though. If the school has an orientation for family members, your attendance will show that you value your student's experience. In addition, the program will give you information that can help you support your son or daughter. Other ideas for showing your interest:

- Schedule a checkup on the car to be sure it's in good shape.
- Cut back on your student's chores and responsibilities at home; college is more demanding than high school.
- Celebrate the successes and acknowledge the hard work throughout the year to show that you respect your child's academic efforts.

The best advice from experienced commuter students is for students to make the trip to school and find parking *before* the first day. Even if they've made the trip to campus many times, they may not have driven the route during rush hour or tried to find a parking spot when all the lots are full. An upperclassman tells incoming freshmen to drive the route to school at least twice before school starts, including once at the time of day they will be going to campus. "My first day, it took me more than an hour to get to school, and it's usually only a half-hour drive," he said. "Somehow I missed the exit, and I ended up in the middle of downtown rush hour. I was ready to go home and drop out of school before I even got started."

Students should also develop multiple backup transportation plans in case their primary plan breaks down. A minor accident might mean no car for a few days, but students still need to go to class. A transit strike requires alternate transportation. A car pool only works if all drivers cooperate and all riders are ready on time. Occasionally students will have odd hours—a group project that requires a 9:00 p.m. meeting or a lab experiment that takes longer than anticipated—and buses may run at different times or along different routes at night.

QUICK TIPS FOR STUDENTS

- Master the practical skills. Be certain you can do your laundry, iron a shirt, and replace a missing button. If you're a commuter student, or if you'll be taking a car to campus, know how to change a tire, where to get an oil change, and what to do if you're in an accident or stopped by the police.
- Don't save packing for the last minute. If you arrange your belongings by categories and do it a little at a time, it won't seem so massive.
- You'll probably have doubts at some point during the summer. "Did I pick the right major? Is this the right school? Maybe I should go to the same college as my best friends after all?" You picked your college for a reason, and you were admitted because the school believes you will succeed there. Don't second-guess

yourself. If it really is the wrong place, you can transfer next year.

- If you'll be living on campus, get in touch with the person you'll be rooming with. You don't need to talk for an hour, but ask a few questions, tell your roommate something about yourself, and see what happens from there. A text or email is often easiest for a first contact; arrange an in-person meeting if the distance isn't too great.
- Prepare yourself to ask for help, and you'll get it. Every college has faculty and staff who can talk to you about what classes to take, how to get along with roommates, and who can answer your questions.

SECTION 2
Early Days

CHAPTER 3

Reality Bites

Establishing New Patterns

Despite all your planning and preparation, the only sure thing about your student's first day of college is that it will be unpredictable.

When we took our oldest son to college, I was certain that we all were ready for this step. We packed our two cars for a leisurely three-day road trip/vacation from Minnesota to Houston, Texas. With our two sons in one car and my husband and me in the other, we started our 1,300-mile journey south. We carefully planned meeting points for gas, meals, and hotel stops along the route so that we could change drivers and make sure the vehicles were both running well.

After arriving in Houston and finding the residence hall, we watched our son check in at the front desk. The student worker on duty welcomed him and gave him his room key, a booklet of residence hall rules, and a two-page handout on bright yellow paper, covered with bullet points and bold type. "These are your hurricane instructions," I heard him say to my son. "You might have heard there's a hurricane just off the coast. It was supposed to hit land farther east, but now they're saying it could come ashore near here sometime during the night. If it does, we'll be knocking on doors to get everyone up and moved into the hallway."

I had been confident our son was prepared for everything he would need to know for college, but hurricane survival tips had never entered my mind. We hadn't paid much attention to the news on our way south, and a pending storm was not on *my* radar. I stepped up to the desk and said, "I've been reading all the information the university sent us, and there was never any mention of hurricanes. He's from Minnesota. He doesn't know about hurricanes."

"It's okay, ma'am," the student said. "We've got this. We've been through it before."

This tall, lanky kid, who obviously would be tossed around like a toothpick in a strong gust of wind, was supposed to protect my son from a hurricane?

As hard as it was to accept, I had to recognize that things would happen during the next four years that I had never predicted and my son wasn't prepared for. I needed to trust his judgment, and I needed to have confidence in the staff at this university. As they reminded us at the parent welcome, fully trained, professional, and caring advisers, safety officers, and student services personnel were on duty around the clock to deal with not only the typical problems that college students experience, but also any emergency situations that might arise.

HOW WILL ALL THIS STUFF FIT INTO A DORM ROOM?

Throughout the summer, college is the future—something to look forward to and prepare for. Once students start packing the car, though, it becomes real. A father described his son, loading boxes into the van, suddenly turning to his parents and saying, "I'm not ready. I know I've got all the stuff I need, but it's me— *I'm* not ready."

Some students genuinely *are* ready, but most students are on edge. Talkative teens become silent as they get closer to their college town. Quiet students chatter nervously. Arguments develop over minor points. A mother recalls driving the width of Pennsylvania in silence while her daughter fumed that packing the car had taken too long, and now her roommate would get the best bed. One year, when I was helping move students into a residence hall on Move-In Day, I watched as a car pulled up to the curb. The freshman in the front seat nervously scanned the scene of people hauling boxes, laundry baskets, and pillows across the lawn. He opened his door, stepped to the back of the car, and threw up.

Students aren't the only ones who are anxious and emotional. Parents are stressed, and anything that fails to go as planned serves as evidence that they should take their child right back home. The father who finds a line of people waiting for the elevators will be convinced that the dorm is an architectural labyrinth and utterly unsafe. A mother who sees a box-elder bug on her daughter's windowsill will capture it in a plastic bag to prove to the hall staff that the room is not habitable. As student services professionals remind each other, parents' anger, sadness, and fear stem from the same underlying feeling: "I want my kid back."

Although parents can't prevent their student or themselves from being nervous, they can help make the move-in process less traumatic. The last thing your child wants on Move-In Day is for the family to stand out. While you may think you're being supportive by wearing a bright new T-shirt in the yellow and black school colors, your daughter would much prefer that on this, of all days, you quietly fade into the background in nondescript khaki.

Mothers and fathers can take heart, however, that their student is already beginning to see them as more acceptable parents than some of the alternatives. Although your son may seem shockingly embarrassed by you on Move-In Day, he also is noticing that you're not nearly as bad as the family making all that noise in the room down the hall.

So what is the recommended plan for Move-In Day? Do you arrive at the earliest possible minute, unload your student's belongings at the curb, and drive away? Do you plan to stay for the weekend to make certain that your child meets at least one new friend?

The first suggestion is to take the most direct route to campus. Many parents, especially fathers, like to think that the one thing they can do for their child on this last "family weekend" is to plan a nice, leisurely trip with a stop along the way for a hike, a picnic lunch, and maybe a side trip to a ball game. Your student, however, is not in the mood for a vacation. He is intent on getting to school. Your efforts to give him a memorable send-off will be unappreciated.

If you must do something to keep your mind off your child's departure, put your energy into fussing over the car rather than trip planning. Have it washed, vacuum the trunk, get the oil checked, replace the windshield wipers, check the tires. Any maintenance that prevents a breakdown is a good investment in family harmony. A first-year student stuck on the side of the road, in a stuffy car filled with her family and every one of her most valued possessions, is a sure candidate for an emotional meltdown.

Soon enough your daughter, lugging a carton topped with her comforter, will walk into the room that will be the center of her life for the next eight and a half months. The focal point, the bed, will look stark and uninviting. As she drops the box on the floor and tosses her comforter onto the plastic-covered mattress, you will see a mix of excitement and disappointment on her face.

"I thought it would be bigger," she might say as she looks

around. "Two of us are supposed to fit in here? Those are really small closets."

Living in a residence hall is a constant exercise in adaptation, and unpacking is the student's first step in learning to make do. For parents, Move-In Day is a pop quiz in the art of relinquishing responsibility. Your son or daughter will not approach the process as you would. This task, however, belongs to your child, and you must help only when you're asked.

Your student will appreciate assistance carrying things up to the room, and most students accept your offer to make the bed. As one young man noted, "I think that was the only time my bed was made all year."

Depending on the student's own technical ability, some are happy to let a parent or sibling help set up the various electronics and put together anything labeled "requires some assembly." Beyond that, though, students usually prefer to do their own unpacking in their own time. Tempers grow short when a parent suggests which drawer the socks should go into or where the family photo should be placed. And this is not the time to remind your child that you warned her all this stuff wouldn't fit in a dorm room.

Younger brothers and sisters are intrigued by this new place, envious of their older sibling, and often at least a little disconcerted by the prospect of leaving their big brother or sister here. A burst of jealousy is common as the younger child demands attention. Steph recalls her twelve-year-old brother insisting the first thing she should unpack was her new microwave so that he could make popcorn. To stop his fussing, she dug the microwave out of the pile of boxes and let him plug it in. As she focused on arranging her closet, her brother managed to scorch the popcorn, sending out waves of smoke and an offensive smell that lingered not only in her room, but through the entire hallway for the rest of the afternoon.

When your student shows signs of irritation, it's usually best for the family to take a break. The college may be offering a family reception for parents and siblings. A visit to the college's art gallery, a campus tour, or a nearby tourist highlight will give you something to do while your student makes decisions about where things will go. Give him time to do some unpacking and, with luck, he'll meet a roommate or the neighbor across the hall while you're gone. Parents are relieved when they come back after a break and see that their child is feeling more comfortable and self-assured.

You can offer to take your child out for a meal or make a run to the mall for last-minute items, but let him decide if he wants to go. Some students are not ready to say good-bye yet and will appreciate time with their parents while they think through the next steps. Others refuse any suggestion to get back into the car. Either way, it's hard for students to consider this as cozy family time.

If you've traveled cross-country to bring your student to school, you may be planning to spend some time in town before heading back. I've known of parents who booked a house rental for a week so they could make sure their student was okay. Please note: this is definitely not recommended. Students have work to do during the first few days at college, even if classes don't start for another week. They want to meet other students, and they need to follow the college's schedule for first-year students. If they arrange their meals and free time to be with their family, they will miss opportunities to connect with other students and start exploring campus.

Parents wonder when and how they should take their leave. "Is there some sign I can watch for that tells me she's ready for me to go?" There is no magical sign, although some students will help you out by saying, "Go. Please. Now."

No matter what, though, eventually you do have to leave. As

one residence hall director bluntly explains, "It's like that old song says. 'You don't have to go home, but you can't stay here.' We don't have room for parents."

Your child will be grateful if you avoid sentimental farewells in front of the roommates. Most students find this step less difficult if they walk their parents to the car to say good-bye. All you need to say can be summed up in a few words. "I'm proud of you—I love you—I know you'll be fine." If you're convinced you won't be able to drive for all the tears, just go a few blocks until you're out of sight, and park the car for a while.

On the way home, take some time to celebrate your own success. You've reached a family milestone. Most parents have some favorite tunes their student never lets them listen to in the car. Scientific fact: singing releases endorphins, which raises the spirits. Exercise and chocolate release endorphins as well, so take that hourlong hike you skipped on the way to campus or stop on your way out of town for a hot-fudge sundae. Then sing to your heart's content all the way home.

When you arrive home, keep the celebration going. Curl up with a book you've been meaning to read. Treat yourself to a bouquet of flowers or a great meal. Take a long, hot bath. One couple opened a bottle of wine from the year their student was born. You deserve some self-indulgence. Within forty-eight hours, though, get in touch with your student.

Some parents believe that the "distance" their student needs when they begin college means they should wait for the child to make the first phone call. Although students probably don't want their parents to call every night, and they certainly don't need to hear daily reports about how empty the house seems, they do want to know their family is thinking about them. One student, Larissa, remembers that her roommate's mother sent a short text message every evening and shipped a package of cookies or brownies once a week for the first month. Larissa's own mother always sounded happy to hear from her daughter, but she made a point of saying that she would not be one of those interfering mothers who call all the time.

One day Larissa called to tell her, "I have to say, I'm beginning to feel a little neglected here! You never call. Randi's mom sends treats all the time, and she says she's willing to adopt me. I'm about ready to take her up on the offer."

A text, brief email, or a quick phone call just to say hello is not an intrusion. And no matter how glad they were to see their parents leave on Move-In Day, very few students object to receiving photos or packages from home.

THE COMPLAINT DEPARTMENT

All the college and university websites that students looked at when they were researching schools captured the idealized image of campus life: golden autumn days with students gathered in front of red-brick buildings or lounging with their laptops on a grassy lawn; jubilant fans decked out in matching T-shirts at a basketball game; a student gazing into a microscope under the watchful eye of a benevolent professor.

While nearly all students will have moments that resonate with those idealized images, they will also have times when absolutely nothing goes right. They have to complain, and the people who will hear first about their terrible, horrible, no-good, very bad day are their parents.

In most cases, the first days at college usually turn out to be a relief. Things may not be as perfect as students had imagined, but neither are they as bad as their worst fears. People are pretty nice, the dorm room isn't as cramped as it seemed that first day, and when a problem arises, there are people on hand to help. Students manage to figure things out. There is almost unreasonable happiness in discovering that their student ID actually opens doors and pays for snacks on demand.

Before long, though, the joy fades. Fall semester for freshmen is a roller-coaster ride of ups and downs. Although they come to school expecting new experiences, they can't possibly predict the impact of all that they will encounter.

- They will almost never be alone. In most families today, children have their own bedroom, and many have their own bathroom. In a residence hall, they may share an efficiently compact room with one or more people, and they will almost certainly share a bathroom—in some cases with ten or more people.
- There's no accounting for what will drive them crazy. Using the shower after someone else, washing their water bottle in the bathroom sink, or scratchy toilet paper may prove to be far more annoying than crawling over a safety rail to get into a lofted bunk or waking to a roommate's talking alarm clock.
- There is no such thing as a peaceful meal. Even if they like the food, the multiple scents, sights, and sounds of a crowded dining hall become oppressive on a three-times-a-day routine.
- Despite all the activity and opportunities surrounding them, students will experience times of deep loneliness.

THERE'S NO PLACE LIKE HOME

At some point, nearly every freshman will suffer from homesickness. Even commuter students will feel alone or anxious when they're on campus and want only to go home for a while. Feelings of homesickness often creep in during the first or second week of school, but they're more confusing when they show up later. Some students will seem perfectly content during the first month, but then call home weeping in October when they see photos of their high school's homecoming dance. Homesickness may not even show up until it's time to return to campus after Thanksgiving, and the student realizes he won't be able to help string the holiday lights in the yard this year.

Parents don't always know that the emotions their child is expressing stem from homesickness. It sometimes sounds more like anger or disappointment. "This place is not what I expected. They never said the classes would be so hard!"

They may express their unhappiness not as missing the family, but "I miss the dog," or "I can't sleep here. I need my own bed."

Children of single parents express their homesickness as a sense of responsibility. "Are you okay, Mom? I should be there to help with the yard work. Besides, it would be cheaper if I lived at home."

The intensity of homesickness can come as a surprise, especially when these same students have happily gone off to summer camps or extended school trips throughout their lives. Somehow college feels "permanent," not just a temporary respite from home.

Usually homesickness is short-lived. It's a response to being in a new situation without the support system they've always relied on. As students catch on that they can handle their new life, the anxiety will subside.

In the meantime, parents help ease the loneliness by sending messages of encouragement. You might include your student in a weekly family activity—maybe a video call when the grandparents are visiting or a chat while watching a favorite show.

Most important, though, remind your student to get involved on campus. Suggest joining a student organization, getting some exercise, or sharing the box of treats you just shipped. Busy, engaged students don't have time to be homesick.

STARTING OUT STRONG

The routines that students establish during the first three to six weeks of school make a difference between success and failure. These patterns become a part of who they are and how they interact on campus. New students who use time between classes for studying are likely to always identify a schedule for doing homework. Students who go home every weekend in September will probably keep up the pattern in October and beyond. The commuters who hurry home after class every day during the first few weeks may never find their own niche on campus.

College students are usually in class only 15 to 18 hours a week. The expectation is that for every hour a student is in class, another two to three hours should be reserved for studying. A class schedule of 15 credit hours, then, represents a weekly time commitment of 30 to 45 hours outside of class. Students who revel in their unscheduled time and postpone writing papers until the last minute or who pull all-nighters to cram for tests will not be as successful as they could have been.

It's not only what students are doing, but how they're relating to their classmates in the first few weeks that makes a difference. Too many students turn to their phones or laptops for a social life, sacrificing in-person companionship. Long strings of texting to a high school friend at another school interferes with building a relationship with the students down the hall. Online gaming consumes hours, interferes with studying, and may turn into an obsession.

Listen as your child describes campus life during the first few weeks of classes. Within a couple of months, students should start to feel like they belong. Commuter students should be staying on campus most of their day, not only for classes but also doing homework and meeting with other students and instructors. Students who live on campus should be dedicating blocks of time for studying during the day and in the evenings.

The first semester is a transition period. All students will vacillate between being thrilled to be in college and wondering if they might rather be home, but you should see progress in their adjustment. At least one class should be challenging enough to talk about; at least one instructor should be engaging enough to merit attention; and at least one friend should be worth telling you about.

Mini-Calendar of the First Six Weeks

Day 1—An emotional day for everyone in the family. Students are tense, excited, scared. Parents are on edge; if anything goes wrong, they may find themselves reacting more strongly than they would expect. Advice for parents: Remember that this is just the first day. You and your student are dealing with a new situation, and it helps to recognize that most things are going just fine. You can handle the glitches.

Week 1—Social acceptance—making friends—is the first priority. Students overreact to disappointments and problems. This may be the first time they have had to identify problems and find solutions entirely on their own, without a parent, teacher, or coach to help. They will complain, but they usually manage to adjust. Advice for parents: Be in touch with your student briefly during the first week; enjoy the excitement and acknowledge the disappointments—with reassurance that everything is going to work out.

Week 2—Students may go overboard with new freedoms. They figure out that attendance is not taken in classes, and they decide not to go. They see other students decorating their rooms, and they spend a small fortune on posters and pillows. Advice for parents: Listen for clues that your child might not be making the best decisions. Affirm the good choices and talk about priorities.

Week 3—A combination of comfort, excitement, and uneasiness confuses students. They have established a routine, and they no longer feel "new." They become extremely close to friends they've just met. They can't believe they've known these people—their best friends in the world—only a couple of weeks. On the other hand, students are frustrated that there is obviously so much they don't know yet about college. Any mistakes feel like proof they don't belong. Advice to parents: Every time you talk to your son or daughter, you are likely to get a completely different image of how things are going. The next time you talk, see if the message has changed.

Week 4—Students who have not yet gone home might want a weekend away from school. The intensity of it all can be exhausting. They begin to see things from a slightly different perspective— the gregarious, outgoing friend they met the first week of school now seems a bit shallow. The quiet, cynical person next door might not be so bad after all. They get tired of their roommates. They long for a little quiet time, or they want to meet up with their high school friends for a weekend. Advice for parents: Listen to complaints, but don't try to fix things. Suggest that rather than come home for the weekend, they can stay at school and block out some time to sleep or study. The standard recommendation is that students should stay at school until fall break or Thanksgiving.

Weeks 5 and 6: Students react strongly to their successes and disappointments. As they face midterm exams, most find that to some degree college is not everything they had imagined. They have to admit that they've made some poor academic and social choices. Advice for parents: The first semester is all about transition. Change is hard, and your child has probably never gone through such a significant period of adjustment in such a brief period. When your student complains about all that's going wrong, remind him of all the successes you've seen already this semester.

COLLEGE CULTURE SHOCK

First-year students are subjected to every possible warning and piece of advice about safety, social interactions, and academic success. Residence hall staff talk about fire drills, cooking regulations, nighttime security procedures, and alcohol and drug policies. Student affairs staff stop by to talk about getting involved on campus, developing leadership skills, and making smart choices about finances and health. Academic advisers give tips on time management, study skills, and how to avoid plagiarism.

Meanwhile, there are new words and new traditions that students are expected to somehow know—the University of Michigan freshman is confused when her classmate says to meet at the Fishbowl at 3:00 p.m. to work on their group project. At Wake Forest, students are expected to "Roll the Quad" after the team wins.

College also presents first-year students with all kinds of new experiences, small and large. The suburban high school grad who is going to school in a big city can't fathom life without his car. The farm girl from North Dakota is puzzled to see people carrying umbrellas on her Boston campus. "Do people really use umbrellas?" she wonders. "I thought that was something only the British do."

Where she comes from, if it rains you either stay indoors until it stops, drive where you're going, or wear a hat.

New information is firing in from every direction, and hardly any of it is hitting its mark. First-year students are not looking for advice or wisdom. They're looking for friends. But friend making is one of those skills no one ever thought to teach them.

Friendships, in their experience, just happen. If they grew up in a small community, their parents knew the families of all their friends. In cities and suburbs, their friends were the kids next door or at their after-school programs. Neighborhood schools and private academies usually draw students who share similar backgrounds, and most of their friends are much like themselves. Friends they meet online most likely share a common interest, or they've been introduced by a mutual acquaintance.

In college, students don't have family references for the people they're meeting. Proximity plays a major role—they live on the same floor, have a couple of classes in common, or just happened to sit at the same table for breakfast and started talking. Then students have to figure out not only who will be fun and interesting, but also who will be trustworthy. In their urgency to have a friend or a date, many students make uninformed choices and then don't know how to break off a relationship.

Students who are not naturally outgoing can feel like outcasts. To them, the icebreaker games that seem to be a requirement at every social gathering are painful exercises in forming fake friendships. It seems like college is designed for the extroverts of the world, and shy students are expected to magically turn into perky, approachable socialites.

Students of color can feel particularly isolated. If they went to a high school where diversity was the norm, they may find they are a distinct minority on campus or the only person of color in their psychology lecture hall. College was supposed to provide an intellectual environment where race and culture don't intrude, but it seems like they're often expected to speak for their entire race on complex philosophical or political matters.

Most colleges have a wide range of student organizations,

including culture-based student groups, to help students meet, receive support on campus, and celebrate diversity. Although students settle in comfortably over time, initial feelings of difference and separation can be particularly difficult in the first weeks of school.

FRIENDSHIPS: TRUE OR FALSE

The friends that students make in their first year on campus can be the most positive—or the most damaging—influence of their college years. Students are vulnerable to bad relationships when they're lonely or homesick, when they've recently broken up with a boyfriend or girlfriend, when they're bored, and when they're struggling academically or financially. Social groups and clubs might promise connection—or salvation—but then pressure students to confine their relationships only to members of that organization. Students might be required to prove their commitment through initiation ceremonies and hazing. Athletic teams, social organizations, or even the college band sometimes challenge students to perform demeaning acts—even deadly behaviors—all in the name of fun and friendship.

Years ago, hazing was viewed as a harmless prank. It was justified as a way to ritualize and build bonds between members of a group. For those doing the hazing, it was amusing, and for those being hazed, it was seen as a way to prove their loyalty. But the balance of power between upperclassmen and new members can lead to degradation and abuse. When students are subjected to sleep deprivation, servitude, physical or mental abuse, or overconsumption of alcohol or even of water, they are in danger. Colleges and universities promote zero tolerance on hazing, but hazing still happens. If parents have any indication that students are being victimized, encourage them to contact the group's adviser, the dean of students, campus police, or if it's related to a fraternity or sorority, the group's national chapter. For more information, see stophazing.org.

The easiest time to build healthy relationships is when students are doing something they love. Whether it's sports, music, biking, shopping, or a passion for the same video game, friendships have a chance to grow when people have something in common.

As important as it is to find friends with similar interests, though, "different" does not equate with "bad." Except for the smallest private schools, colleges and universities introduce students to a world of new ideas, new cultures, and new activities. Students between the ages of eighteen and twenty-two are receptive to learning, and they're in an environment that supports them as they open their minds to new people and new experiences.

QUICK TIPS FOR STUDENTS

- The first day of school, you are not the only one who doesn't know what's going on. All freshmen are scared and confused. Some of them simply hide it well.
- If your parents are irritable on your first day at college, it's because they're nervous, too. The fact that you're starting college is almost as big a change in their lives as it is in yours.
- You will encounter some disappointments about college. Don't expect college to be a four-year vacation package. Your dorm will probably not be a five-star hotel, the dining center won't feature the menu of a Michelin-star restaurant, and you can't expect a daily schedule of entertainment options.

- Get up, get out, and get involved, even if you're the kind of person who prefers to melt into the background. Turn off the laptop, ignore social media for a while, and meet the people across the hall. Say hello to the person sitting beside you in class. Talk to the person next to you as you go through the cafeteria line. Someday, one of those people will say, "I am so glad you came up to me that first time!"

- The way you feel today is not how you'll feel tomorrow. You will have days when you're not at all sure you know what you're doing, but you'll also have days when you know things are just fine. Remember the good days so you can draw on them during the tough ones.

- Be willing to rethink your choices. You can drop friends who don't turn out to be what you expected; you can change majors; you can change your sleep, diet, social, and study habits if they're not what they should be. The best part of being a freshman is that for a whole year you can say, "I'm still trying to figure things out."

- For commuters, the adjustment to college is at least as challenging as it is for students who live in a dorm. Spend your free time on campus, make a space there for yourself, do something to get involved, and start to think of college as your "real life."

CHAPTER 4

Distance Parenting

Mentoring Through Technology

From infancy through adolescence, children test and expand their levels of independence, sometimes with their family's blessings and sometimes against their wishes. At least once during high school, and certainly during that senior summer, your child must have declared, "You can't tell me what to do. I'm not a little kid anymore." And now it's true. When students are in college, parents really can't oversee their "emerging adults" on a daily basis.

Although you have much less direct control, you still have influence. For the next four years, you will be parenting from a distance, which requires greater trust from you and greater competence from your child.

If parents have studied psychology, they will recognize that the steps they go through as they adjust to their student's college transition tracks Maslow's hierarchy of needs. The psychologist Abraham Maslow said that certain basic requirements (food, drink, shelter, and sleep) must be met before we can move on to satisfying other needs.[3]

Parents track through the stages of Maslow's hierarchy as they

---

3. A. Maslow, *The Farther Reaches of Human Nature* (New York: Viking, 1971).

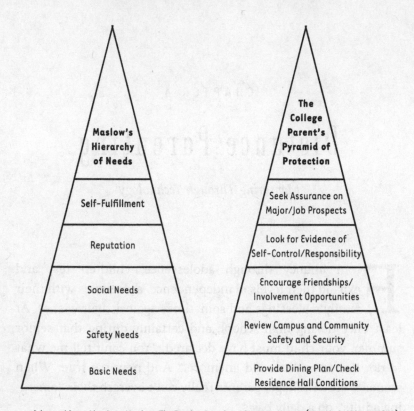

Adapted from Abraham Maslow, *The Farther Reaches of Human Nature* (New York: Viking, 1971).

gradually release responsibility to their sons and daughters. They carefully study residence hall information so that they know their child will have a comfortable place to live. They compare meal plan options to be sure their child will eat well. On Move-In Day, they do a safety check—they flick light switches, look for alarms, sprinkler systems, and the nearest emergency exit, and they test the locks on the doors.

When families go home after settling their student into the dorm, they may be ready to trust those baseline measures, but they still want ongoing assurance that everything is in place. They will continue to ask, "Are you eating all right? Is your room okay? Are you getting enough sleep? Make sure you walk with someone when you're out after dark." And they want to know about their student's friends.

Students may get tired of the questions, but parents feel compelled to hear the answers. What parents really want to know is, "Can you take care of yourself?"

Soon parents are moving to the next level of Maslow's hierarchy as they begin to worry whether their student's major is a good fit and whether it will lead to a job. And finally the question is whether this whole college experience is worthwhile. Is their student getting the value from college that will serve her well in her next stage of life?

Although parents work their way up the pyramid over time, they periodically return to the basic needs. When their student moves into her first apartment, they will want to know if she can make her own meals and how safe the neighborhood is. It may not be enough to hear that the apartment is safe and there is food in the refrigerator; parents may need to see the evidence. Then they look for assurance that the roommate relationships are supportive. The process continues throughout the college years and long beyond as adult children face new decisions and experiences.

I'M PAYING THE TUITION! WHY CAN'T I GET THE BILLS?

Eighteen-year-old college students are considered to be adults— except, of course, for all those times when they are not. If you think it's confusing for you, look at it from a student's viewpoint. The college tells him that he is an adult. He's responsible for his own decisions and for all of his debts. Then they remind him that he can't legally drink until he's twenty-one. If he's caught drinking, the school might call his parents to "discuss his behavior." His financial aid is based on his family's income. And at any time, his parents can provide proof that he's financially dependent on them, and suddenly all his privacy is gone.

Throughout a child's elementary and high school years, the federal Family Educational Rights and Privacy Act (FERPA) ensures that parents have access to their child's academic records and, at the same time, protects those records from public scrutiny.[4] When students enroll in college, however, their records become their own. Grades, financial information, disciplinary action, and even the number of credits a student is taking are all protected and confidential. The school will not release information to anyone, including parents, without permission from the student.

Residence hall staff and judicial affairs professionals might encourage students to talk to their parents about conduct issues, but they won't discuss problem behaviors unless the student gives approval. And what FERPA doesn't protect, HIPAA (Health Insurance Portability and Accountability Act) does.[5] Medical personnel and psychologists cite HIPAA when they explain that they cannot tell you what treatment your student is receiving or even if he's had an appointment at the clinic.

The obvious complaint—and college administrators hear it every day—is, "I'm the parent. I'm paying for my child's education. Why can't I get any information about his bills or his grades?" You can—with your child's permission or by submitting your federal income tax forms, proving that you claim your

---

4. United States Department of Education, "Programs: Family Educational Rights and Privacy Act," https://www2.ed.gov/policy/gen/guid/fpco/ferpa/index.html (accessed July 14, 2019).

5. United States Department of Health and Human Services, "FERPA and HIPAA," https://www2.ed.gov/policy/gen/guid/fpco/doc/ferpa-hipaa-guidance.pdf (accessed July 14, 2019).

child as a dependent. Most schools make the release process simple, telling parents how their student can grant access to family members. Some schools, though, may not mention privacy until the parent calls complaining, "I haven't received a statement yet for my daughter's tuition. How much do I owe?"

Always, though, students have access to their own information and can give it to their parents.

You may wish the school would simply hand over your student's records, but most parents and educators recognize that there are good reasons to honor student privacy. A student should have the right to prevent a noncustodial parent from receiving personal contact information. Colleges and universities do not know if the person seeking information is a trusted family member. Stalking and harassment can result from access to personal information. Colleges and universities will not assume that every family member is loving and caring, because, unfortunately, some are not.

INFORMATION IS POWER

Today's students recognize the high cost of a college education, and they appreciate their parents' investment. They're accustomed to turning to their family for guidance, and they continue to want family support as they work their way through school. Even so, parents are likely to encounter defiance when it comes down to precisely which information their student will share. Your son will be happy to give you the tuition bill, but he's hoping you won't find out that he's taking only ten credits this semester. Your daughter needs you to cover the copayments for her medical appointments, but she doesn't want you to know why she went to the emergency room at 2:00 a.m. last weekend. You feel like you're always hearing only half the story.

During Family Weekend, a college counselor offered assurance to the group of parents who were gathered for brunch. "You probably are noticing that your sons and daughters aren't telling you everything they're doing, and they're not showing you every grade they receive. There's a reason for that.

"A major developmental task at this point in their lives is to develop independence. They're trying to figure out how to separate themselves from their family and from their friends, and at the same time, how to keep a healthy connection to you. An important part of developing this level of autonomy is deciding which information they will share. The separation process may have begun at birth, but you're still cutting the umbilical cord eighteen or nineteen years later. Step by step you and your child are working on establishing 'appropriate boundaries.'"

To parents, these boundaries seem less like fences than a complicated maze. Your child will allow you to come just so far into her life, but the moment you ask a question about her new boyfriend or the state of her finances, you will find an impenetrable barrier. "I've got another phone call. Sorry, I have to go."

If you back up and wind your way down a less direct path, letting her lead the way through your conversation, you might find that she's not only telling you about this new boyfriend, she's suggesting that you should meet him. She may not tell you the precise balance on her savings account, but she might mention that she's made a spreadsheet for tracking a monthly budget.

Your student controls the information you get, partly because of data privacy restrictions, but mostly because she *is* growing up, and she wants to figure things out on her own. Your questions can conflict with that self-governance. Still, there are things you do need to know, such as when tuition is due. Or when to pick her up for spring break.

Counselors recommend that parents ask questions that cannot be answered with a simple yes or no. Once students start talking and are convinced that their parents are listening, not judging, they will share as much information as feels comfortable. Some ideas for conversation starters:

- Ask open-ended questions that show interest in your child's experiences but don't require intrusive details. Instead of "How are doing in your Spanish class?" try "Tell me about your Spanish class." Rather than "What did you do last weekend?" ask "What do most students do on the weekends?"
- If your child doesn't seem to want to talk, you can carry the conversation for a while. Mention things that you know interest her. If she participated in high school sports, tell her how the team is doing. Talk about the family pet. Tell her the news at home—like the security system upgrade or the recent storm that blew through town. Just as you need an image of your student's life on campus, she needs the occasional update of how things are going at home.
- Avoid judging. Students are sensitive to any hints of disapproval or criticism.
- If you need to ask about finances, student records, or other specific information that your student considers personal, keep that part of the discussion separate from the rest of the conversation. "Before I say good-bye, I wanted to mention that I'll need your grades from last semester. I have to provide your transcript to keep your 'good student discount' on the car insurance."

In the best of situations, your child will give you the information you need, even if the message is not all that you might wish. Because students don't want to disappoint their family, though, they will work hard to prevent their parents from seeing poor grades, finding out that they did something foolish, or hearing that they're in serious trouble. Almost everything you hear from your student will be filtered through the best possible lens. Sometimes students will be vague about what's happening in their lives, and sometimes they will flat-out lie.

When you hear a story that doesn't seem to ring true, consider whether there's something your child might not want to acknowledge. If you hear that the college doesn't post grades, you probably have a clue that there are academic difficulties. If you hear about a new, hundred-dollar midterm registration fee the college just added, it may be an indication that your child has had some kind of expense she doesn't want you to know about.

A discussion at the start of college, plus occasional follow-up conversations, can establish what kind of information you need and which topics can be considered private or discretionary. Your student is unlikely to share details of every quiz or expenditure, and you will not hear about every party or date, but parents are justified in asking for general information on academic performance, the social scene, health issues, and bottom-line financial balances.

If you don't show an interest in your student's education, she will think you don't value how hard she's working. If you show too much interest, she will think you don't trust her. Parents struggle with the fine line they must walk, but the path is smoothest when they express frequent recognition of their child's efforts and successes. When students see that their parents use information to provide support rather than assert control, they end up offering information because they want to, rather than because they have to.

HOW MUCH COMMUNICATION IS TOO MUCH?

Families are unsure how often they should be in touch with their student. There are no rules, and there is no "norm." Some families talk on the phone once a week or less, but they may be sending texts daily. Some students call home every day—or more than once a day—and send selfies on a regular basis. For other families, an occasional phone call is enough. How often families are in touch is not necessarily an indication of a healthy family relationship, nor is it a sign of dysfunction.

What matters are the reasons for the communications. If the calls and messages are quick notes on the day's successes or brief stories your student thinks you'd enjoy, it's probably not a problem to get a couple of texts, a five-minute phone call, and a photo or two in a single day. If every call or message is a list of complaints, though, or if your student is asking for your help on each decision she makes, someone needs to put the brakes on. Students are at a point in their social and emotional growth where they should be making their own decisions and finding support outside of the family network. They still need your advice and understanding, but they should be relying on themselves and turning to people on campus—friends and staff—to work through most college issues.

The immediacy provided by communication technology is both a blessing and a curse. Parents and students are communicating more and better than ever, but if parents call and get no answer, or if they text and don't receive a response within a couple of hours, they worry. An email that doesn't elicit a reply within a day can raise an alarm. The student, however, may have turned his phone off during class and forgotten to turn it back on. Maybe he was doing countless other things and hadn't checked that particular email account in a couple of days. Or maybe he glanced at his list of messages and thought, "A message from

Dad. I'll read that later," and he just didn't get back to it. Some parents insert code words into the subject line of an email or the first few words of a text when they need a response. One family has agreed that urgent messages will begin, "Respond Now."

Sometimes it's the parents who are calling multiple times a day. If that happens, ask yourself, "Am I doing this for me, or for my child?" The empty nest can lead a parent to check in with their son or daughter every time they set the table or pass the vacant bedroom and feel a sense of loss. It's like reverse home-sickness. You're lonely for your absent child. Just as we encourage students to get busy and get involved, the same advice goes for parents—join something, plan something with your neighbors, and make some new friends.

The best part of "high-tech communication" is that it has created some "high-touch" rewards. Students and parents find that emails and texts make it easier to say things to one another that they can't say in person or over the phone. Sometimes the lack of visual and verbal cues can make for more affectionate communication. As they write a message, there are no interruptions and no body language or voice inflections to interfere. Email users frequently disclose far more than they would in person, much as a blogger confides more to an invisible audience online than she does in person.

"I hate talking on the phone," one father said. "I don't like small talk. With a phone call, I feel like I have to have something important to say. But if some little thing pops into my mind, I can send an email or text, and I figure my son will read it when he has the time. Yesterday I was eating lunch at my desk, and I sent him a message telling him, 'I'm sitting here at work, eating your favorite kind of sandwich, and I'm thinking about you. You're a great kid, and I'm lucky to be your dad.' I'm not the kind of guy who would ever call and say that to him."

Multiple technologies create more opportunities for different kinds of communication—a brief text message just to check in; an email with a list of the latest news items from home; a lengthy phone call when you know you both have some free time; a video chat after dinner. Students say they tend to use different kinds of communication for different members of their family. One student explained that she usually calls her mother, but she emails her father. She and her sister text all the time. And every couple of weeks she sends a card or letter to her grandmother, because her grandmother prefers mail—and sends stamps.

WHEN THE GOING GETS TOUGH, THE TOUGH CALL HOME

Parents are the sounding board for every complaint. You will hear about tasteless food, unfair homework assignments, inconsiderate roommates, and impossible-to-understand instructors. The worst calls are the Midnight Meltdowns. As one professor explains, "When the sun starts to set, small problems feel much more serious. Offices are closed, and as the night grows darker, students are sending multiple anxious emails to professors. Then they wake up their parents with 2:00 a.m. phone calls."

The next morning, the Parent and Family office on campus is hearing from exhausted mothers who couldn't get back to sleep. "She called in the middle of the night, and she was so upset. I don't know if I should bring her home or just stop answering the phone after midnight."

Parents are miserable when their child is unhappy. In most cases, though, when your daughter has purged her frustrations—and as the eastern sky begins to glow with the first signs of returning light—she will decide she can talk to her instructor before class, and she goes to bed. Or after your son unloads his problems on you, he sees his across-the-hall neighbor on the way to the vending machine, and they spend an hour putting together a basketball dream team. In the meantime, you don't know that your child feels better. He doesn't call you back the next day to say the problem is solved. And if you call him but get no answer, you only worry more.

In most cases, students aren't calling because they expect you to solve their problems. They're trying to decide if the situation really is a problem and if they have to fix it. As they talk through the situation, they're finding the words to describe what happened. They need sympathy. Life is more challenging than ever before, and all this problem solving is hard work. They're recognizing that they probably caused or at least contributed to the issue. After they've vented their frustration, they'll be ready for the next step: figuring out a solution.

AM I HELPING OR HELICOPTERING?

If you believe the news stories and media reports about parents of college students, you are probably convinced that your parenting peers are all intrusive, demanding, and prepared to protect their child at the expense of all other students. You know *you're* not like that, but apparently everyone else is out of control.

In my experience, the vast majority of parents are reasonable, thoughtful, and all-around decent people. I've certainly seen some parents who are genuinely overinvolved or inappropriate in their relationship with their student or with the college, but the numbers are small.

Parents become involved when they're afraid for their student's educational well-being, their safety, or their life. They call because they don't have the information they need to answer important questions.

The worst-case scenario is not the hypervigilant mother or father. College administrators, residence hall staff, and campus advisers are skilled at dealing with complex situations and difficult people, and they can handle those conversations. The worst case is when a mother or father *doesn't* get involved when a student genuinely needs help—because they're afraid of being tagged as a helicopter.

An out-of-state father called on Move-In Day one year to report that his son had gone for a bike ride after hauling everything up to his room, and he'd had a bad fall. He had a broken leg, and he was in surgery. The doctor said he would have to be in the hospital for at least a couple of days.

"I won't be one of those helicopter parents," the father insisted. "I'm going to stick around tonight, just to make sure he's okay, and I'll probably unpack a few things he didn't get a chance to put away. I'll go back home tomorrow. I'm just calling to ask if there's anyone who needs to be notified that he's in the hospital."

"We can work out the notifications," I said. "But your son is in the hospital, he's having surgery, he hurts, and he's just arrived in a new city. Stay as long as you can. He needs you right now. That's not helicoptering, it's parenting."

Avoiding the Helicopter Label

The difference between being supportive and being intrusive is not always clear. Before intervening in your student's problems, consider the following:

- Can most students your child's age handle this kind of situation on their own? Is there some reason your student cannot handle it? Unless there's a *really* good reason, let your student do the work. "Being busy" or "having a test" do not qualify as good reasons.
- Will your student learn something by handling the situation? Students gain important knowledge and skills by

solving problems, and they meet the people who can help them now and in the future.

- Does your student want you involved? Often students talk through an issue with their parents as a way to test their plan and figure out how to discuss what's happening. Listen, then step back.
- Will your involvement complicate matters or make things worse? Students can lose face or appear weak when their parents step in.
- Do you have the full story? If your student has the details or records related to the situation, it doesn't make sense for you to try taking control. Relaying information back and forth takes time and causes confusion.

You should be involved when:

- Your student is unable to communicate. You may not be able to fix the problem, but you can relay information to those who need to know of your student's situation.
- Your student has physical or mental health issues that prevent making well-informed decisions.
- Your student's financial mistakes are likely to affect the family finances.
- You cannot locate your student.

If you do need to step in, keep your involvement minimal and frame your questions in a way that provides direction to what your student needs to do, not what you will do.

Different colleges have different approaches to working with parents. Some proactively deliver messages to parents about campus services, timely topics, and upcoming deadlines. Some identify a contact person or an office that parents can call for answers to their questions. Many schools regard parents as partners with the college or university and as advocates for their student's education.

As mentioned earlier, data privacy restrictions limit the information higher education institutions can legally provide to parents. While college personnel can't necessarily tell you specific details about your student, they can talk about policies and procedures. If you want to know why your student is on academic probation, they can't tell you what your student's grades are, but they can tell you the conditions under which students are placed on probation. They can't tell you if your student has been sanctioned for underage drinking in the residence hall, but they can tell you what the policy is for dealing with underage drinking.

Some parents assume that commitment to privacy works both ways. Residence hall staff and student services personnel get calls from parents that begin, "I don't want my son to know that I called, but can you tell me . . . ?" In most cases, university staff can't promise to keep your concerns secret, and students aren't easily fooled. If a resident assistant unexpectedly knocks on the door to check on a student's well-being, that student will guess that someone has alerted the staff person, and parents will be the first suspects. Usually staff tell parents that they can check on their student, but they would prefer to say, "Your parents asked us to look in on you. Is everything okay? Is there anything I might be able to help with? How about if you just give your mom and dad a call?"

When you're concerned about your student and you're looking for some insights, you probably have your own full circle of experts to consult. Your friends who have children in college can give you an opinion based on their family's experience. A recent college graduate who works with you might understand what your student is going through. A niece or nephew a little older than your child may be able to offer a helpful perspective. Talk with the people who know your child and who have some recent experience with campus life.

Still, sometimes you do need to guide your student in finding help, and the assortment of campus offices and advisers can be confusing. "How do students know who to talk to?" a parent complains. "For every single thing that comes up, it's a different person or office."

What's more, with just about every transaction or service being offered online, parents wonder, "Where are the *people*? Are there any actual human beings my kid can talk to?" Although most questions can be answered through email or by directing students to the right website, personal contact is still the heart of student services. Based on the question, the person your student can contact should be clear:

- *Academic issues:* Students can talk to their instructor if a concern is related to a specific class; otherwise students should talk to their academic adviser.
- *Residence hall issues:* Students can first talk to the resident adviser (RA) who lives on their floor. If the RA can't help—or seems more like a friend than an adviser—the student can talk to the hall director. For disturbances or illegal activities in the residence hall, students can report incidents to campus security or police.
- *Commuter issues:* Some schools provide an office for commuter students. If that's not the case at your student's college or university, the counseling office or the student's academic adviser is probably the best resource.
- *Personal issues:* Students can visit the school's counseling office or academic adviser.

- *Physical and mental health issues:* Students should make an appointment with a medical provider at the school's health center, counseling office, or at a local clinic. Walk-in appointments are often available.

If your student is truly unsure about how to proceed with a problem, suggest asking the closest "authority figure" she can find. It might be residence hall staff, an academic adviser, or an instructor. If the first person doesn't have an answer, tell her to ask someone else. In almost every case, she should have a good lead by the time she has talked to two or three people. Someone will direct her to the right office or the best expert.

QUICK TIPS FOR STUDENTS

- The college or university you attend regards you as an adult. That means you own your educational records. Unless you make other arrangements, the bills will come to you. If you expect your parents to pay the bills, make sure they receive them!
- If it seems like your family wants too much information, talk to them about the kinds of information you will share (maybe general updates on your financial standing, health issues, overall academic progress, and an overview of the social scene) and what you would prefer to keep private (the grades you get on quizzes, daily personal expenses, and details about your dating life).
- When things go wrong, you may be tempted to call home and turn the problem over to your parents. Before you call, try figuring out what the problem really is, what steps you can take, and—if you need their help—exactly what kind of help you are asking

for. Parents are reassured when their student has done
the initial troubleshooting and has worked out a plan.

- Sometimes parents want to solve problems for you.
  Practice saying, "It's okay. I've got this." Use that line
  politely anytime you need to.
- If you do not call your parents regularly, at least send
  a quick email or text. They need to hear from you
  from time to time to know you're all right.

CHAPTER 5

Home Fires

College Is a Family Affair

Family structures and patterns develop based on all members of the household. When one person is absent, it's not just the physical presence, or the humor, or the affection that is missed. It's also the role that the person plays in the family.

Thea's parents expected life to be quieter after she left for college, and they knew they were going to miss her. She was the family storyteller and drama queen. Every night at dinner, she had at least one tale to tell, and she could stretch out an entertaining description of her day and all its disasters through the entire meal.

What they didn't expect was that their younger daughter, Marissa, would become so difficult after Thea left for college. They assumed that at age fifteen, Marissa was well past that challenging adolescent stage. They were caught off guard when she melted down every evening, storming out of the dining room before they finished eating.

With Thea gone, the family had lost its lightning rod. When even the mildest friction arose in their family, Thea would draw attention away from the issue and toward herself. Now that tension had nowhere to go, and Marissa didn't know how to handle it. The family was going through a significant adjustment, and Marissa's behavior was just one of the results.

OUT OF SIGHT, NOT OUT OF MIND

Within the lifetime of today's students, technology has added a new component to family transitions. Back in the day of once-a-week phone calls from an absent college student, there was no question that students were out of the house and on their own. Now it's no longer clear when a student actually *leaves*. It's hard to acknowledge that a son is gone when texts constantly pop up reminding parents that the boy needs money or advice. Parents sometimes feel like they know more about their child's daily life in college than they ever did when the student was at home, and they struggle to figure out how to let go when their child is still hanging around virtually.

Allison never expected her daughter to tell her quite so much about her life at school—not just stories about her roommate and classes, but details about what she was eating for every meal, the squirrel she saw on the way to class, and when her period started and ended. She finally told her daughter, "Honey, it's probably best that I don't know *everything* about your life. Really . . . too much information." When the calls continued multiple times a day, Allison felt she had to set some limits. "No more phone calls when I'm at work, unless there's an actual emergency. How about if we plan on talking every other day for a while? You can text, but don't expect me to respond right away. I'll get back to you if it seems like it's necessary, but let's just try a little less conversation."

In spite of the virtual connections, families manage to develop new patterns and schedules when a child leaves home. With only one or two people gathering for dinner, it might seem unnecessary to set the table and have a formal meal. The traditional Sunday night pizza-and-TV schedule turns into your time to make the weekly grocery run.

Some of the changes that college brings will feel like a gift. You get your car back, or at least you don't lie awake every Friday night listening for the sound of the garage door. The brother or sister still living at home is receiving extra attention. Morning schedules are less hectic. If your last child just left for college, you and your partner can talk about sex anytime, even at the dinner table.

On the other hand, without your child as the center of your attention, you may find yourself feeling lost and lonely. It's not unusual to "mourn" for a while when a child leaves home, and it's not entirely coincidental that parents' midlife crises correspond to their children's college years.

The dissonance caused by a child's departure can result in one parent rejoicing, "We can change everything!" while the other protests, "We've had enough change! Can't we leave things alone for a while?"

The harder one partner pushes for change, the harder the other pushes back for stability. Transition is a process, not an event. Patience will bring transformations to both partners—over time—more successfully than demands for immediate upheaval.

At some point, you may find that you feel a touch of envy for what your child is experiencing. Countless parents look at their student's new life and say, "I wish I could go to college. Someone would fix my meals, I could take any classes I want, I would have no obligations, and I could have intelligent conversations every day. Why do we waste all this on kids?"

You're stuck with your responsibilities, but you can still expand your mind. This is the best time in your life to do the things you've been putting off—take a class at a local college, train for a half marathon, concentrate on improving your career, volunteer at the local animal shelter, or pamper yourself (and your partner). As your new life develops, you can look for ways to adapt and create new routines. Depending on your outlook, all the changes forced on you might seem somewhat depressing, or they can feel rather daring and exciting. As one father from Florida noted, "People talk about the 'empty nest' like it's a bad thing. I don't feel like I'm living in an empty nest. I feel like a 'Freebird.'" Then again, you might be oblivious to any particular differences at all until the first time your student comes home for the weekend, expecting everything to be the same, and points out that you've gone rogue. "We always have pancakes and eggs for Saturday breakfast. What's with the cereal boxes on the table? This just feels weird."

When students come home and find life even a little different, they feel unsettled. They knew *they* were changing, but they had assumed the family would stay the same.

"I talked to you almost every day. You could have *told* me you changed the Wi-Fi password."

They also don't know how these changes may affect them personally, and there's a clear line between what they can grudgingly accept and what feels like an attack on their territory. They still don't want you to turn their bedroom into your exercise or craft room.

Students find comfort in returning to the familiar, and they rely on the stability of "family." They'll let you know they are surprised—maybe even disappointed—at some of the differences they see. Nevertheless, they adjust. They go back to school and tell their friends, with pride and amusement, that their mother signed up for ski lessons, their father went snorkeling for the first time, or Grandpa sold his car and bought a scooter.

THE SINGLE-PARENT FAMILY

If the college transition creates challenges for two-parent families, the dynamics for one-parent households can be greater yet. Amanda knew her life would be different when her son went to college, but she wasn't worried about *his* adjustment. She had raised him to be independent, and he seemed to face every problem with logic and patience. The sense of loss they both felt when she left him at college surprised her.

"When we were saying good-bye," she recalled, "he asked if *I* was going to be all right. He said if it got to be too much for me or the younger kids, I should call him. He said he'd come home every weekend if I wanted so that I could have a break.

"He shouldn't have to feel that kind of responsibility! And I shouldn't have been so tempted to take him up on the offer."

Children growing up in single-parent families take on roles that create huge gaps when they leave home. The oldest child is the family babysitter and makes sure the younger children do their share of the housework. An only child or the last to leave home becomes more like a friend than a child every year. They're the extra hand when help is needed, and they're the other side of the conversation at the dinner table.

As college students, they feel ongoing responsibility for the household. They make choices at college based on concerns about the family. They turn down study abroad opportunities, because that would mean being too far from home. They come home every summer, rather than staying on campus, in order to take back the lawn-mowing or cooking duties. They even pick careers that will return them to their home community.

For a single parent seeing their last or their only child settling in at college, there are powerful, complicated feelings. There's the well-deserved pride that you've succeeded at this task of parenting; you've reached the goal you've been striving for all these years. At the same time, though, a major identity in your life is no longer paramount.

New complications can flare up as ex-partners, sometimes including new partners, weigh in on college choice and the student's academic goals. Finances may have to be renegotiated, along with emotional decisions on where students will spend holidays and breaks.

There can also be new opportunities. When their children start college, single parents can make changes they didn't believe they could consider before. A new job, dating, or just spending more time with friends all seem possible again.

Soon after her daughter started college, Tammy talked with a financial planner about quitting her secure computer programming job to go back to school herself. "He told me I could do it. It will just take two years, and I'm still young enough to have a whole new career. He said I don't need to worry that I might be spending all my retirement funds. With me in school, my daughter will actually get a better financial aid package, and as a 'returning student' myself, I qualify for some scholarship funds, a campus job, and I'll have an adviser who specializes in working with older students."

COMMUTER FAMILIES: LIVING WITH CHANGE

When any student enters college, the sphere in which the family operates will expand to include the college or university. For families of commuters, the student is bringing elements of that new community into the house every day. A college student's schedule is extended from morning until late into the night, which means the family's daily routine is directly impacted. Social expectations for young adults are different than for high school students, and those, too, filter into family functions.

Parents may be willing—or even want—to know more about the courses and the demands their commuter student is dealing with, but at this age, young adults are at a developmental stage where they need to be less connected to their family. Even the simplest questions can seem like prying. Parents can hardly avoid asking, "How was your day?" "Will you be home for dinner?" "Do you need the car tonight?" The questions seem conversational or logistical to parents, but students interpret them as meddling.

It's fairly common for commuters to keep their campus life private. Life is easier if they don't have to explain and justify the details of their day. They don't think their parents will understand how college works, and they're not even sure they understand it themselves. Like everyone else their age, they've seen the films and TV shows, and they know their experience is not mirroring the media image of college. Commuter students believe their classmates who live on campus have more fun, more freedom, and more friends than they do. To some extent, they're right. Although they *can* have the fun, explore the freedom, and meet the friends, they have to navigate college differently when part of their daily routine includes a mental and physical transition from home to school and back again.

That doesn't mean that family members should avoid asking about school and providing encouragement. Just about every college student can identify one or more people—usually a parent or family member—whose support has been key to their persistence and success. When parents let their student know that education is a family priority, the student's determination to succeed increases.

- Encourage your student to stay on campus between classes and to participate in clubs and organizations, attend athletic events and concerts, and take part in social activities. The more time they're on campus, the more likely they are to feel that it is "their" school.

- If your commuter student works, encourage her to get a job on campus. Even if wages are less than she can earn off campus, the support of college-based supervisors and the time at school are beneficial.

- Read campus news and be alert to the school calendar. Ask your student to explain things you don't understand. If you acknowledge the importance of what's happening at the college or university, your student will, too.

- Attend any family events on campus, especially parent/family orientation, Family Weekend, and graduation. Don't skip orientation because you visited campus during the college search. What you'll learn at orientation is what you need to know as you prepare your student and yourself for the first days of college.

SOMETIMES THE TRUTH HURTS

At some point, you will probably have to report some bad news to your student. Over the four years that a student is in college, it's almost inevitable that a major family event will occur. A grandparent may die, someone could be diagnosed with a serious illness, or the family pet may need to be put to sleep.

During Ava's junior year, her parents made the decision to divorce. Traveling together from Chicago to Ava's school in Seattle in January was out of the question. They had to tell her over the phone. With both parents on the call, they said they had some difficult information, and they were sorry they couldn't be there to talk in person. They told her that both of them had agreed they wanted to divorce. They promised to mark all her life celebrations as a family—graduation, marriage, the birthdays of any children she might someday have. They asked for her questions and listened to her cries and her anger.

Delivering difficult news is challenging, whether you call, write, or show up in person. Parents worry if their child doesn't seem to react.

"I had to call and tell my son that his grandfather had a heart attack, and he might not make it. And my son just said, 'Well, tell him I said hello.' Then he said he was walking into class, and he ended the call."

Students facing new and difficult situations don't react in predictable ways. If you encourage your child to "talk about it," she'll say something completely inappropriate or won't say anything at all. Parents complain, "I don't think she actually heard what I was saying." Meanwhile, their student has scouted out a good friend and repeated every word her parents said with astounding recall. Your child hears you; she just doesn't know how to respond.

When you must deliver bad news long-distance, plan on checking back in a day or two. Give them time to digest the information. Let them know that they can call you whenever they want. And if they react poorly, don't judge. There is no right response to bad news.

QUICK TIPS FOR STUDENTS

- Your first trip home might be a surprise. You will probably find that things have changed. Keep in touch so that you won't be blindsided by your father's shaved head, the yoga mat and exercise ball in the family room, and your mother's new diet, which means there are no more carbs in the house.
- Call, email, and text with brothers and sisters still at home. They may not say they miss you, but at least

sometimes, they do. If you treat them well, they'll watch out for your interests and your room while you're away.

- If you complain to your family about everything that goes wrong in your world, be sure to let them know what's going well, too. They want to hear about your successes, and they are among the few who will truly, deeply share your pride.

SECTION 3
College Culture

CHAPTER 6

Credit Loads and GPAs

Adjusting to College Academics

T he overarching purpose of college, from the parent perspective, is for students to have a safe environment to
grow emotionally and gain knowledge in preparation for a
future career. The reality of college, though, is that it's a lifestyle.
Academics and out-of-classroom experiences blend together for
the full college canvas. As counselors are fond of pointing out,
the most important thing a first-year college student can learn is
self-management.

Those students who have grown up with the most structured
lives often bask in their newfound freedom. No one is telling
them what to do. Left alone to plan their days, they finally have
a chance to listen to podcasts for hours on end, jump at every
social opportunity, or lie in bed and stream videos endlessly.

This freedom comes at the same time students are faced with
new and different teaching and learning methods, the need to
make new friends, and more responsibility than they experienced
in high school. It's no wonder the first semester is sometimes
disastrous.

ACADEMIC EXPECTATIONS

All his life, Jackson planned to go to the university that his parents had attended. The family lived just an hour away from campus, and every year they bought alumni season tickets for football and basketball. As an infant, Jackson was the photogenic baby in the crowd wearing a miniature school sweatshirt. His high school wardrobe was made up mostly of T-shirts and caps featuring the college mascot. As a first-year student, Jackson made sure all his friends knew the words to the school songs, and at football games, he helped the cheerleaders fire up the student section. When he met his parents for dinner after the games, they were pleased to see him feeling so comfortable in the student union and at all the traditional campus hangouts.

Jackson had earned mostly A's and B's in high school, and his parents had no doubt that he would do equally well at college. They were totally unprepared when he told them in January that he was on academic probation.

Their son had seen only the social side of college throughout his life, and he never considered that his classes might be more difficult than he was prepared for. When his parents had talked about their college years, they always focused on memories of athletic events, parties, and the spring break trip they took with friends when they were seniors. It was only after learning that Jackson was on probation that they told him about the hard work and dedication they had both put into college.

"You know, Jackson," his father said, "we *did* go to games and parties in college, but we treated weekend socializing as a reward for studying. And there were times when we didn't take any time out for fun.

"I still remember the weekend when I had to choose between going to the last football game of the season or studying for a statistics test. It was killing me because a win would mean we would qualify for a bowl game. But I had to study because I was right between a B and a C for the course. I really needed an A on the test.

"I stayed home from the game to review everything we'd learned that semester. I studied most of the day and then gave myself the reward of watching the last quarter on TV. I would have loved to be at the game, but I knew the coursework came first."

GOOD INTENTIONS, BAD ADVICE

It's easy to see why students prioritize their social life over academics. They've been hearing from relatives and all their family's friends that "college is the best time of your life." When they arrive on campus knowing no one, and every day presents new and mystifying problems, it's far from reassuring to think that life will never be better than this. These are times when it's almost refreshing to have a pessimistic grouch in the family who will say, "I wouldn't go back to your age for anything. All those doubts, questioning every decision you make, the daily problems? Trust me, kid. Life gets better."

Parents want their children to enjoy college, but they also want them to use this time well. They try to provide guidance as their child selects courses and navigates coursework, but with every good intention, parents sometimes offer some of the worst possible advice.

If parents attended college themselves, they're thinking back to their own experience, but college is not like it was a generation ago. The way classes are taught, how students learn, and the support services they can access have all changed significantly. Still, they want to help their children avoid the mistakes they made. They urge their students to select a prestigious major as incoming freshmen, test out of introductory classes, and get all their general education requirements out of the way as quickly as possible. As a result, students end up feeling overextended and lost in challenging classes that are beyond their comfort level. Or they're frustrated by coursework they don't care about.

Parents who didn't attend college are mystified by the vocabulary and the range of class structures: labs, lectures, discussions, seminars, independent learning. If their student can sign up for online courses, they wonder why campuses even exist.

Student success research indicates that first-year students are happiest when they have a mix of large and small classes.[6] During the first semester, students should take at least one class for skill building or pure enjoyment. Colleges and universities support this idea by offering freshman seminars, small classes that connect first-year students with a faculty member. The course might concentrate on strategies for student success, or it may be a cutting-edge science course on new technology, an analysis of a presidential campaign during an election year, or a course on happiness. The underlying outcome is that the student will be studying with other first-year students and thoroughly investigating a topic taught by an instructor who is enthusiastic about teaching it.

Foreign-language courses also provide a way for students to connect with one another in smaller classes that meet multiple times a week. Students are required to speak in class, working in pairs or small groups to practice conversational skills. Instructors ask students to talk about personal experiences—family, their community, how they celebrate holidays, and what they did over the weekend. Vocabulary and grammar improve as students search for new words and try to form sentences. They begin to see that mistakes are not fatal and that everyone slips up from

---

6. R. Light, *Making the Most of College: Students Speak Their Minds* (Cambridge, MA: Harvard University Press, 2004).

time to time. They learn more about their classmates through their conversations, and they often register together for the next semester's class, extending their friendship beyond a single term. An extra bonus is that language classes provide background and incentive for study abroad opportunities later on.

GRADES—THE MEASURE OF SUCCESS?

College is an entirely new environment for students, and the personal standards and measurements from high school no longer apply. As a junior and senior in high school, John's goal was to earn no lower than a B in any class and always to have more A's than B's. His first semester in college, though, his highest grade was a B-plus, and he had a C in his required English class.

Despite all the talk of "grade inflation" at college—the awarding of higher grades to appease students and make schools look better—some professors stress that a C means the student is doing what is expected. B's and A's are reserved for the students who go beyond the basic requirements of the course. Parents should allow some leeway for slightly lower grades, especially during the first year of college, and promote the concept of "doing your best" rather than "being the best."

If you notice over time that your student's poor marks are coming from one area of study—maybe your son is doing well in English and history, but the math grades are low—it could be that his high school courses were not up to the standards of this college's math department. Or perhaps he registered for a higher-level course than he should have. Maybe his learning style didn't match the teaching style for the class. A pure lecture class, for example, can be difficult for students who do better with interactive or visual learning. The free-range, creative writing that earned an A in a high school English class may be judged as too unfocused for a college essay.

Most colleges provide tutoring for students who are struggling with skill-level challenges. Although there may be a cost involved, one semester of tutoring can give students a boost not only in the work for a particular class, but also in learning how to study for college courses. A school's Learning Commons, usually connected with the college library, will offer individual assistance, study-skills workshops, writing labs, information on note-taking techniques, and exam preparation. Students can ask a librarian to review their research methods as they begin working on their first college paper.

Counseling and advising offices also provide information for students on study techniques. Some offer student success courses, individual coaching, online resources, and multisession workshops on learning strategies. Students with documented learning disabilities can receive accommodations for note taking and test taking.

Most new students hear the message, "Talk to your instructors!" Unfortunately, that's difficult advice for a first-year student to follow. Freshmen are trying to appear confident, and one of their greatest needs is to avoid drawing the wrong kind of attention to themselves. If they go into their professor's office, they wonder what they could possibly say that would improve their class standing. "If I ask questions, I'm just putting my instructor on notice that I don't get it."

Some advisers suggest that first-year students ask an instructor *any* question, even if the student already knows the answer; conversations and relationships can begin from the most simple and awkward start. Others will tell students to ask a general question, such as "How did you first get interested in this topic?" Or they can just say, "I know I'm supposed to talk with my instructors. I don't really have any questions, but I'm here. How does this work?" The bottom line is that all the evidence indicates that students who talk to instructors—or seek help from advisers and counselors—are the most successful and the most likely to complete their degree on schedule.

CAUTION LIGHTS

Even the best students will come across a course during their college career that seems particularly challenging. It may require skills they don't yet have, or it's simply not "their" course. Some students will never be able to pass calculus. The rudiments of organic chemistry may never make sense. Sometimes a student just doesn't connect with an instructor. The occasional bad grade is not an indication of serious academic trouble, but a continuing trend of progressively lower grades or an entire semester of below-par performance are signs of a problem.

Naturally, parents react strongly when they learn that their student is failing. When you're spending tens of thousands of dollars each year for your student's college experience, low grades are alarming, especially if they're coupled with the possibility of probation or expulsion. Parents can hardly avoid being upset if they find that they've paid for a year or more of classes that have no value to the student.

When students are struggling academically, most parents will either demand change or advise their student to "try harder." According to students, however, the last thing they need to hear from their family is "Shape up! Get to work! You can do this."

"If only it could be that easy!" they moan. "Being told to 'shape up' doesn't help."

What's more, if the student is using the wrong study method, working harder while using the same method is not the solution. On the other hand, when poor grades are caused by poor choices—partying too much, sleeping too little, socializing too much—the fix is self-evident. The student *does* have to shape up. The issue then becomes whether or not she wants to. Most colleges and universities are intent on providing a good education, but their primary purpose is not to enforce mature behavior or force a student to do her homework. Neither you nor your student can expect the college to monitor your child's lifestyle and ensure her success if she's not willing to make the effort herself.

There are obvious times when difficulties are likely to occur. First-year students start college with great confidence—after all, they spent all of high school preparing for college, so they must be ready. But the first graded paper or quiz can be a reality check. "I'm not sure I should be at this school. Does everyone else know what's going on in that class?"

Rarely does a student, even the brightest and most organized, go into midterm exams feeling entirely prepared. For first-year students who have never experienced the stress of college exams, the fears are far worse.

From midterms until the end of the semester, the tension slowly grows. Professors set deadlines for major papers or projects right before or right after Thanksgiving break. As a result, students start the week of Thanksgiving with misgivings, and their worries only increase as they try to find time to pack and finalize travel arrangements. Then, heading back to school after the long weekend, they worry that they made little or no progress on that paper—who can study with family and friends demanding attention? The December days leading toward final exams are stress-filled as students try to balance all their end-of-semester responsibilities. Students have accused colleges of blatant cruelty for scheduling finals at the worst possible time of year—just when they need to buy and wrap holiday gifts, pack to go home, empty out the mini fridge, and clean their room for pre-break room inspections.

The process repeats during spring term. A hopeful start to the semester turns into tense days leading to midterms and spring break. Their return from a weeklong break triggers the anxiety of project deadlines. Then final exams come just as warm weather and fresh spring breezes tempt students to abandon their books for a last chance at fun with friends before summer separates them.

From year to year, new challenges crop up. The second year of college brings a sophomore slump when the excitement of college has waned. Before the end of the sophomore year, they're expected to declare a major, squelching the dream that "I can do anything I want!" Those who were convinced of their career goals as entering freshmen now are wondering whether they dare switch to some new interest.

The semester when a student moves out of the residence halls is a significant adjustment period, and grades often drop. The joy of sharing an apartment with three best friends or living with three dozen sorority sisters evolves into disagreements and tension, and students realize there's a difference between quantity and quality of friendships.

For juniors, classes become more demanding as students get into their majors. From the second half of the junior year through the final year of college, stress increases as students see the "real world" creeping up on them. "I need to find an internship. Why did I major in classical civilization? I'm never going to get a job. What was I thinking?"

Times of transition are typically accompanied by academic difficulties, but a drop in grades also may be an indication of personal or social problems. Academic struggles can be a symptom of health issues. Lower grades may signal problems with roommates or a boyfriend or girlfriend. Students who have been sexually assaulted may be able to project an outward calm, but their grades can suffer as a result of their inner anxieties.

Poor grades might also accompany financial problems. Some physical and mental health conditions first manifest during late adolescence—in other words, during the college years—

and affect all aspects of life. And anytime students are examining their career choice and questioning the direction they have selected, they are likely to suffer academically.

As mentioned earlier, there are times when family members should contact university staff if they see their student struggling. The classroom relationship and academic issues, however, are matters that should remain between the student and the instructor. Parents don't help their student by calling a professor to complain that a grade was unfair or ask for an extension for a paper.

College is a time when students should be speaking for themselves. By now they should be capable of talking with authority figures without help from a parent. If they're not yet ready, this is the time to learn those skills. When you're tempted to intervene, take a moment to consider first how your student can grow by doing this job himself. Then ask yourself what would happen if your spouse or partner—or your own parent—made a phone call to your boss about a problem you were having at work.

College students are not entirely on their own. Higher education institutions have strong support services in place. They have appeals processes to guide students through disagreements, whether the complaint is with a faculty member, a housing official, or a registration process. At small colleges, staff members and academic advisers know their students and can offer guidance as they see problems developing. At larger universities, students may need to ask for help rather than wait for someone to offer it, but even more resources are available.

TRANSFER STUDENTS: SAME SONG, DIFFERENT VERSE

More than a third of college students today transfer to a different college or university before graduating. For some, transfer is written in the stars from the first day on campus—a two-year or community college is designed to start students along the higher-education pathway, then send them on to the next step. For others, transfer becomes an option when things don't work out as planned. The student who never expected to miss home so much, the health sciences major who doesn't have the grades to get into the selective nursing program he had hoped for, or the student whose health condition requires attending a school where he can get the treatment he needs—any of these students may choose to change schools. And sometimes transfer is not merely an option, but a mandate. The student who is expelled for violating campus policies or who fails to meet academic standards may find himself seeking another route to a college degree.

When Mingzhi's parents learned she wanted to transfer to a new school, they were frustrated about starting the college search all over again. "She got into her first-choice school, and she really liked it there, but at the end of her freshman year, she decided she wanted to major in nutrition. Her school didn't have a nutrition program, so we're back where we started."

While many steps in the college search are the same the second time around, there are some new factors to consider. Will the coursework from the first college transfer to the new one? If the credits count, do the courses fulfill requirements for the major? If there was a specific problem at the first school, does the new one have services to prevent the same issue? And students need to be willing to make another transition to a different campus. It is a significant adjustment process to start at a new school and make connections all over again.

Transferring should not be regarded as a simple solution to a correctable problem. A relationship gone wrong, poor grades, residence hall problems, or not feeling connected during the first few months are all challenges that can be overcome without changing schools. The general advice is that dropping out mid-semester means a needless loss of time and money. Students are encouraged to stay for the first full year—or at the very least, finish the first semester. When problems arise, it's usually better for the student to talk through frustrations with an adviser than jump to another school.

Certainly, there are good reasons to change colleges. Parents may hear only "It's not working out. I want to transfer." You can best provide support if you know the underlying reasons, but students may not entirely understand—or want to admit—what those reasons are. Some questions to ask:

- What isn't working at their current school? If they can articulate their concerns, they will know what they don't want next time around.
- What *is* working? What do they like at their current school? This is helpful in deciding whether it makes sense to stay, and equally helpful to keep in mind if they need to select a different school.
- Do they want to go somewhere else, or are they planning to drop out of school completely? If they plan to continue at a different school, they will need to make decisions and begin the application process as soon as possible—while continuing their coursework at their first school. Or they may want to take time off while they decide what's next. If so, what will they do during that time?

When students—like Mingzhi—opt for a major that is not offered at their starting school, they have no choice but to find another. If family financial circumstances or health concerns dictate that the student must be closer to home, or the student genuinely does not fit in with the culture of the college, transferring can be the best option.

But transferring is not always a seamless process. Even with an associate's degree from a two-year or community college, students can lose credits and fall behind. A student who is preparing to transfer should start with a conversation with the advising office at his current school to find out if they have agreements—called articulation agreements—outlining how credits transfer to other colleges or universities. The next step is for the student to meet with a transfer admissions specialist from the college or university the student is considering. The more details that students can work out in advance, the more successful the process will be.

One issue that is sure to come up as students start at a new school: Will they find friends? Mingzhi complained to her parents, "Everyone at my new school probably has all the friends they need." Her parents reminded her that she had made friends at her first school by introducing herself to her classmates and by ushering for theater performances. As it worked out, on the first day of class the instructor in her nutrition class asked for volunteers for a community service project, and Mingzhi raised her hand. Within three weeks, she was staffing an information table at the local farmers' market, alongside new friends who shared her interest in wellness and nutrition.

GRADUATING IN FOUR YEARS—OR MORE

Students plan on completing an undergraduate degree in four years or less, although some career-based bachelor's degree programs require an extra year. Many students have earned college credits during high school that allow them to finish college in just two or three years. A few colleges and universities are offering a three-year curriculum, with classes offered year-round and no summer break.

In fact, only about 40 percent of college students graduate

within four years. Nationally, around 60 percent of full-time, first-year students will receive their degree within six years.[7]

Colleges and universities typically follow a standard format—15 or 16 credits per semester over eight semesters of study for a minimum of 120 credits. If students earn those 120 credits, and if they take the *right* courses, they will graduate on time. More often than not, though, something will interfere with that plan. An illness, failure to complete a critical requirement, or an overly challenging course might convince a student to drop some credits mid-semester. A family crisis may call the student back home. Dropping one too many classes can lead to delayed graduation. Adding a minor or a second or third major will require more credits and more time.

During the college selection process, the admissions office looked carefully at Audrey's application. Her high school grades were slightly above average, and she was a student council member and class treasurer. The acceptance committee's conclusion was that she was a solid, well-rounded student, and she should succeed at this school.

The first semester, Audrey registered for 15 credits, but she dropped her biology class after deciding she was "not awake enough at 8:00 a.m. to be using sharp and breakable lab equipment." The second semester, she again enrolled for 15 credits, but her French III instructor suggested that she withdraw after she did poorly on the first three quizzes. "Since you didn't take French last semester, you seem to have lost some of your high school language skills. Start with French II next fall or get some tutoring during the summer, and you'll be able to catch up, no problem."

7. "College Completion Rates Are Up, but the Numbers Will Still Surprise You," NPR, 2019, https://www.npr.org/2019/03/13/681621047/college-completion-rates-are-up-but-the-numbers-will-still-surprise-you.

Although she completed only 11 credits each of her first two semesters, Audrey still had trouble keeping up with her coursework. She ended the year with C's and C-minuses.

After talking to her academic adviser, Audrey recognized that the study habits that had worked for her in high school were not sufficient for college courses. Cramming for exams might have helped her pass the multiple choice tests in high school, but the essay exams in political science required a deeper understanding of the material.

Audrey's parents began to see that the four-year college plan they had anticipated was not on track. In order to succeed, she would first need to put some time into mastering basic study skills. A lighter course load for her sophomore year, supplemented by tutoring and academic counseling, brought her up to speed and improved her grades. She managed to graduate in five years with an acceptable grade point average of 2.8.

When students fall behind by a class or two, it becomes increasingly easy to conclude that a four-year plan is out of the question. They put themselves on a five- or six-year schedule without considering the extra cost to their family or themselves. They forget that some grants, scholarships, and reciprocity agreements run out after four years. An extra year of classes isn't just another two semesters of tuition; it also means an extra year of room, board, and other expenses.

As a parent, you can ask for a periodic accounting of progress toward a degree. The number of credits earned is one indication, but more critical is the number of credits still needed to fulfill graduation requirements. Is the student taking the right courses? She may be earning 15 credits per semester, but that doesn't ensure she will graduate in four years. Every college has seniors with excess credits who still cannot graduate. Students must earn a certain number of credits, meeting specific criteria within their major, as well as courses outside their major. Signing up for an abundance of elective courses is a lot like consuming empty calories. They fill up the schedule without contributing to healthy progress.

As soon as you know your student is falling behind by a class or two, you should discuss how those credits can be made up and whether four-year graduation is still possible. Most colleges and universities have software programs that map out student progress, including steps to take toward graduation. Online classes or a couple of community college courses during the summer might be enough to get back on schedule. If your student is falling too far behind, the sensible option might be to take a year off, work, and develop a focused academic plan.

Few of us really want our sons and daughters to move back home without finishing college, and the goal is to encourage our children to achieve responsible independence. In some cases, additional time with close family supervision will be helpful, but you want to make sure that's the best solution before you suggest it.

WHEN YOUR STUDENT GOES BEYOND YOU

The day will come when you ask about school and find yourself bewildered by the response. "So much fun! My study group is making a video we're calling 'Fenestration of Fritillaries,' and I'm doing the sound track. It's going to be amazing!"

When you express confusion, your child will say, with a hint of condescension, "A sound track—you know what that is. And fritillaries. You know, butterflies. I guess in the simplest terms, my entomology study group is doing a video to explain the angle of that feathery stuff on a butterfly's wings. I get to do the background music."

It's like middle school math all over again, except this time your child doesn't expect you to help. She knows she has exceeded your knowledge base, at least on this one topic. This is the reward you get for supporting her all these years and for sending her to college. Now she can talk down to you.

If you can show enthusiasm about your child's academic interests, you are contributing to her education. It means a lot to a student when a parent asks for more information and shares the excitement of new knowledge. There's no doubt that it can be challenging to show interest in the sentence structure of the Russian language or the characteristics of geriatric bone density. Your admiration for your student's knowledge, though, can spur her to learn more. Plus, as your child explains the subject to you, she understands it better herself.

Ask questions about what she's telling you, and find out why she likes the subject so much. Look up the topic online. Eventually she will come to you for advice on what size lightbulb she needs for her desk lamp. Your status as her personal adviser on all things practical will return, and she'll appreciate your wisdom once again.

Progress Toward Degree

In addition to selecting a major and taking courses that focus on that field of study, a liberal arts curriculum includes courses in the arts and humanities, social sciences, physical sciences, literature, historical perspectives, and mathematics. Students also take coursework that represents studies in civics and ethics, technology, the environment, social justice, and global issues. The purpose is to develop engaged citizens with a broad understanding of society and the ability to work constructively and inclusively with others. Each of the four years of college has its own goals and objectives.

First Year

During the first year at most two- and four-year colleges, students are sampling coursework in a liberal education curriculum. They should be taking a variety of courses representing different subjects and different learning methods. By the end of the first year, students should have discovered some areas of study that excite them, and they should have at least a quarter of their education requirements completed.

Sophomore Year

The second year continues the exploration phase as students work on their general education coursework. The subjects that initially intrigued them are examined more thoroughly as students sign up for increasingly challenging courses. As they consider areas of study, they should be talking to academic and career advisers, as well as faculty, about what the major means in terms of the classes they will take and the jobs they can pursue after graduation. Career planning courses help students explore career interests. If students have not previously declared a major, they should be prepared to make that decision by the end of the second year.

Junior Year

Third-year students take advanced courses in their major. They can visit the career office or the school's alumni center to find a mentor and to explore internship opportunities related to their major. By the end of the junior year, students should have a clear understanding of the range of career options they are considering and some sense of the specific job track they would like to pursue. For some students, the jobs they're thinking about will not be tied to their major. That's not a problem, but students need to be able to articulate how the coursework they've taken has taught them skills, processes, and characteristics that will transfer to the world of work and relate to the career they hope to pursue.

Senior Year

Seniors complete the coursework in their major and finish any remaining requirements and electives. If a senior project, paper, or thesis is required, it should be planned out by the end of the first semester and completed by the end of the second semester. During the first semester, students should visit the career office to explore job openings or graduate school programs. Graduate school exams are usually taken in fall semester with grad school applications due during the fall or early winter. Students should work with their academic adviser to make sure all graduation requirements are fulfilled.

All Four Years

A job search is likely to take three to six months, but some of the work can be done long before the senior year. As students take on student jobs, volunteer projects, or internships, they are learning skills that can be highlighted on résumés. Although a cafeteria job may seem purely menial, students develop customer service and problem-solving skills. The employee who is promoted to "line captain" will gain supervisory experience. A student who volunteers to tutor math students at a local elementary school may be learning about children of other cultures or how to moti- vate underachievers. As students identify skills they're learning, they can include them on their résumé. Examples of success- ful class projects or unique community service projects can be included in a student's portfolio. A senior project often focuses on a unique and interesting topic, and it can attract a graduate school recruiter's attention or be an example to cite during a job interview. Most college career centers offer workshops on how to write a letter of application and provide coaching on interview techniques. Students can take advantage of these opportunities throughout their college years and be a step ahead when the right job opening comes up.

QUICK TIPS FOR STUDENTS

- Remember: Your first priority in college is academics. You do get to have fun, but make sure that classes and homework are covered. It's sobering to realize that every course you're taking costs serious money. When you miss a lecture or skip out of a test, you're actually wasting hundreds or even thousands of dollars.

- If your school offers freshman seminars, take one! They're designed to give you ideas on how to succeed in college.

- Talk to professors. It might be hard, but most professors are teaching because they enjoy working with college students, and they love their area of study.

- When you're confused, when you have a problem, when you don't know what you're supposed to do next, ask for help. There are dozens of people on campus whose job is to help students.

- Career planning begins in the first year of college. If you have a major picked out, talk at least once to a career adviser about your long-term plans. Ask a professor what kind of jobs relate to the course he or she is teaching. If you do not have a major selected, or if you decide you might want to change majors, ask your adviser for help in figuring out how your interests, work style, and personality might fit with some potential jobs.

CHAPTER 7

Picking Up the Tab

Money Counts

Finances are the intersection between family and student, home and college. Love and a lifetime of interactions will keep you connected when you don't see one another every day, but money ensures that you must talk.

No matter how mature and independent your child is by any other measure, financially he or she is still considered your legal dependent. More than 80 percent of all students receive some form of financial aid,[8] and the way federal student aid works, parents' income is factored into award packages.[9] If your child is receiving any financial assistance from you or from a federal loan, it simply is not possible to draw a clear line between your finances and your child's.

---

8. National Center for Education Statistics, "Fast Facts," https://nces.ed
.gov/fastfacts/display.asp?id=31.

9. Students are considered dependent unless they are at least twenty-four, married, a graduate or professional student, a veteran, a member of the armed forces, an orphan, a ward of the court, someone with legal dependents, an emancipated minor, or someone who is homeless or at risk of becoming homeless.

Students manage money best when they have a good understanding of their family's funds. You may choose not to share all your financial details with your student, but the more information parents provide about college expenses, payments, and financial responsibility, the better their students understand the true value of their education.

Unfortunately, it can be difficult to discuss money dispassionately. When Alan learned that he and his business partner would be passing through his son's college town on a job-related trip, he arranged their schedule so that they could have dinner with his son, Joe. The two men picked Joe up from his apartment and took his advice on a campus-area restaurant. The food was good, and the conversation was even better. Joe was enthusiastic about his classes and his friends. He talked easily with both men about his plans for a business career. Alan thought he seemed more mature and confident than he'd ever been.

After they finished dinner and were looking at the dessert menu, Alan remembered the financial aid forms in his briefcase, and he mentioned that he needed a copy of Joe's job earnings and tuition receipts for the past year. "We've got to get those forms filled out for next year's student loans. The good news is, you'll be a senior, and this is the last time we have to do this."

As he spoke, Alan could see his son revert to the sullen and defiant boy he had been at sixteen. Joe slumped in his chair, checked the time, and complained that he had to get back to his apartment. Embarrassed that his business partner was witnessing this unpleasant transformation, Alan tried to change the subject by pointing out the apple pie and chocolate cake on the menu. "Looks like they've got a couple of your favorites, Joe. What do you want?" That only seemed to add to Joe's irritation. "Can I just go? I've got a lot of homework this week."

The mere mention of money is a reminder to students that they're indebted to their parents. Everything they're accomplishing at college, all the pride they take in being self-sufficient, every vision they have for their future depends on a continuing money flow from their family. While they appreciate their parents' contributions, discussions of finances bring back all the unwanted feelings of being under house rules.

Sometimes parents don't even recognize when they're playing the "money card." When your daughter calls to ask for extra funds for a spring break trip with her friends, you might have to tell her that it's not in the budget. You may see this as a simple statement of fact, but to her, it's a message of control; she's not allowed to make her own decisions when you hold all the money.

MONEY MATTERS

Even the most thrifty students will face a financial crisis at some point during their college years. Most students, including those from the wealthiest families, think twice about asking their parents for an extra handout. Whether they overspent because of an emergency, poor planning, binge shopping, or an unanticipated once-in-a-lifetime opportunity, they don't want to explain to their parents what happened and why they need more money.

Between classes, in the study lounge, and anywhere students gather, we hear them brooding over their debts and expenses. Too often, though, a student's focus is on short-term finances rather than the long-term outcome. They fret about getting through the next week or month, although what they *should* be thinking about is how the expenses they're piling up now will affect them through the rest of the year and well beyond graduation.

Financial mistakes can begin before school even starts. When students accept financial aid offers, the instinct is to take out the full total available through grants and scholarships. They may not need all the loan money they're offered. Too often, students borrow as much as they qualify for, but their living expenses or their fees and books might turn out to be less than anticipated. The extra money seems destined for an electric bike or some binge shopping. Borrowed money has to be paid back eventually, and it's better to borrow less now and owe less later.

Parents agree that it is primarily their job, not the college's, to teach their children financial management. Even though families may expect the school to provide guidance and education about sex, wellness, and career preparation, parents say they will take the lead role on money. Because every family's financial situation is different, it really *is* the family's responsibility to make certain their student has a basic level of knowledge about money, savings, budgeting, and indebtedness, based on their own circumstances.

Each year in college presents its own financial challenges. First-year students begin college with a sum in their checking account—in most cases, more ready cash than they've ever had in their lives. They face countless temptations and learn hard lessons in managing bank accounts, debit cards, and the convenience of online shopping. By November, their bank accounts are scraping bottom.

A year or two later, students move into an apartment and find themselves in a financial tailspin. As soon as they settle into their own place, they realize they have to buy a broom and dustpan, trash bags, wastebaskets, and toilet paper. Rent has to be paid on the first of the month, even if they haven't had time to transfer funds. The plan to save money by fixing meals at home falls apart when the scent of breakfast sausage wafts in from the fast-food restaurant down the block.

Budgets need to be revised during the junior year when an unpaid internship, which will be perfect on a postgraduation résumé, causes the student to quit her part-time job in the library. A three-week, three-credit study abroad program might cost the same as a January-term class on campus, but it means airfare, hotel, and restaurant expenses, while the rent still has to be paid on that empty apartment back at school.

Senior year doesn't offer any breaks. Students who are preparing for graduate school have to pay an application fee to each graduate program they apply to, plus a fee for admission tests, and maybe a cross-country flight to interview for a fellowship. Job seekers are taking time off from their part-time work and spending transportation money for job shadowing and interviews. And they must show up in a decent suit and "grown-up shoes," not sneakers or flip-flops. This is also the time when students begin to recognize what their postcollege expenses and student loan repayments will be and how all these debts will affect their future lifestyle.

BASIC TOOLS FOR MONEY MANAGEMENT

The big-ticket items are one aspect of college finance, but the day-to-day maintenance of a college student's budget is quite another. You may believe that you have communicated your financial expectations clearly, but your student might not agree. As Keesha explained, "My parents told me to keep track of my expenses on a regular basis, and they said I couldn't get a credit card. They never told me I needed to write down every tiny little thing I spend money on—it turns out, those add up—and they never told me *why* I shouldn't have a credit card. I mean, *they* have credit cards. Everyone does."

Students have a head start on their future finances if they know how to manage and balance their bank account, understand family expectations about who pays for which expenses, and know how their parents feel about credit cards, debit cards, and mobile payments well before they leave home. Your child already has a sense of how you manage your money—in fact, one of the best predictors of a student's financial problems is her parents' level of debt. Money management, however, is not a subject that can be learned solely by observation or by lectures. Students need practice and skill building.

Jasmine's father asked her to jot down daily spending records at the beginning of her freshman year as a way of helping them both understand what her college expenses would be. For that first month only, he said, he would like her to tell him each week how much she was spending for personal and entertainment expenses. "But please be careful. I'm hoping we've got enough in the budget to cover the whole year."

By recording her expenses during that first month of school, Jasmine saw how quickly the dollars could disappear. After the first week, she had spent more than half of her September budget. When she called her father, she explained that she and her roommate had decided to buy matching quilts and a couple of rugs for their room. She knew when she bought the accessories that her budget would be out of balance, but she had a plan to get back on track. She could begin to make up the deficit by buying juice and snacks from the grocery store to stock her mini fridge rather than using the vending machines in the residence hall. Instead of going out for dinner on Sunday evening, she and her roommate agreed to fix soup and sandwiches in their room. At the end of the first month, she reported that she was still a little behind on her budget, but she assured her father that she would have her expenses back in line within a couple of weeks. He didn't ask again for weekly reports, but at the end of October, she told him that her finances were right where they had planned.

THE CREDIT CARD GAMBIT

A generation ago, most college students had one or more credit cards. Credit cards were easy to get, with tables and kiosks set up at athletic events, concerts, and street corners near every college campus. The landscape today is different. A federal act passed in 2009 targeted deceptive practices by credit card companies and put restrictions on marketing to underage consumers. College students are no longer automatically considered eligible for credit. In order for applicants under the age of twenty-one to qualify for a credit card, they need evidence of a steady income or a cosigner who will guarantee repayment of any debts incurred. But young adults who are taking out a student loan can use that "steady income" from their loans as evidence that they qualify for a credit card.

Despite the 2009 federal legislation, then, more than half of college students today have credit cards. Most families say they want their child to have a credit card in case of emergencies and unexpected expenses. They recognize that online shopping is the simplest way for students to make purchases, and online ordering requires a credit card. When a student studies abroad, a credit card is the best way to manage expenses. By cosigning for a credit card with a low minimum limit, parents have some assurance that their student will have emergency funds if they need it, but parental access to the bills means they can monitor the account. The downside, though, is that if students pay the bills and make only the monthly minimum payment (or less), parents' credit rating can be affected.

PENNY WISE, POUND FOOLISH?

Parents want their students to be responsible about finances and to be cautious about spending. They remind their children to think through their daily decisions related to money. Too often, though, students make choices that will save money, but they don't recognize the real price of their decisions.

During winter break, Nickolas did a budget check and realized he needed to cut his spending in order to make it through the rest of the year. He looked at ways to trim his expenses and saw that the biggest charge on his debit card every week was for groceries and fast food. If he could reduce that amount, he could save a few hundred dollars by the end of the year.

Many students regard food and personal care as the areas where they have the most flexibility. Certainly, students can find ways to reduce expenses, but meals are not the best choice when it comes to saving money. A steady diet of peanut butter sandwiches, ramen, and rice cakes, while cheap, will end up costing too much in energy and health. Late-night snacks and fast-food carry-out can be cut from the routine, but groceries are still a wise investment. Encourage your student to stick with a good diet and find other ways to reduce expenses. In an emergency, many schools have food shelves where students can pick up a bag of groceries at no charge. (By the way, campus food shelves are always grateful for donations from families and friends.)

Few teenagers have a realistic concept of living expenses until they pay the bills. They don't necessarily understand life's basic costs (for example, utility charges, housing expenses, car payments, various insurance fees). They may know those expenses exist, but they don't have a grasp of how it all adds up. They understand best the bills that they themselves have directly affected in the past. They know how much they're spending on music downloads and apps, but they probably don't think about the cost of their share of the family cell phone plan. They know the exact price of a burger and fries, but the weekly grocery bill is a foreign concept.

Students should understand the overall cost of their college education, but such a big sum might seem incomprehensible at first. Some students grasp the situation better when parents explain, "Our share of your college expenses will cost about the same as buying a brand-new car each of the next four years." (At a private college, that might be four really nice new cars.) "Instead, we're hanging on to the old car, hopefully for all four years, and we're helping you pay for college."

You will do your whole family a favor by working through a budget with your child each year. Defining your student's role in finances will help him recognize the importance of working, saving, and making plans to repay college loans. A solid understanding of a budget before school starts will give your student the necessary background to make good decisions when there are choices to be made.

Developing your son's or daughter's financial skills takes time, patience, and perseverance to work through the steps.

- *Encourage—and teach—your student to keep financial records.* Students should understand that it's important to keep bank statements, medical bills and prescription receipts, tuition statements, and receipts and warranties for all major purchases, credit card agreements, scholarship records, and loan agreements. Be sure your student knows that financial records are required for tax purposes and for student loan or scholarship applications. Even if you're paying most of the bills, your student will probably receive the statements and receipts.
- *Organize a file for financial records.* During the first year of school, a single folder for finances is probably sufficient. First-year students can file all major financial receipts and records together. As a general rule, if a folder becomes too bulky to manage easily, it should

be arranged into two or more folders. When a student moves to an apartment, or if he believes that more organization would be helpful, a separate file box for financial records may be needed. Encourage him to get into the habit of filing receipts and statements faithfully.

THE PAYOFF FOR PART-TIME JOBS

College is demanding, and parents don't want their students to take on more responsibility than they can handle. "How many hours of work are too much?" they ask. Balancing academics with a work schedule can become a daily crisis, and family members need to emphasize that school is the priority. Students who are employed more than twenty hours a week tend to see themselves as employees first and students second. When exams or major projects come up, students decide against reducing their work hours if it means a smaller check at the end of the pay period.

On the other hand, having a job helps students organize their time. If they know they have to go to work, they arrange their studying around their job.

The standard recommendation is to limit work hours to no more than twenty hours a week during the academic year.[10] During the first semester, however, students should focus on adjustment and self-management. If they need to work that first semester, they're better off working fifteen hours a week or less

---

10. A. Hess, "Students who work actually get better grades—but there's a catch," CNBC Make It, October 5, 2017, https://www.cnbc.com /2017/10/04/students-who-work-actually-get-better-grades-but-theres-a-catch .html (accessed August 15, 2019).

and taking a job that doesn't require learning new or complicated job skills.

Students and parents tend to weigh the differences between on- and off-campus jobs purely by their pay rates, but jobs on campus have benefits beyond wages. Campus supervisors understand that students can be overloaded at times, and they're usually more flexible about reducing hours during exam periods or when students have major projects due. Depending on the college, campus jobs might provide practical experience related to a student's major. Annaliese, an environmental studies major, found a job with the campus landscaping department during her first year, then was hired to manage the school's organic garden for the summer. Her campus jobs provided practical insights connected to her coursework.

Commuter students especially benefit from on-campus jobs. The work itself can feel like a contribution to the school, and the support systems and connections with other students build a sense of community. On the practical side, having a desk or a workspace provides a campus "home" for commuters. "I had a place to drop my books between classes, and they let me use the microwave and refrigerator, even on days when I wasn't working," Josh recalled. "Best of all, the people I worked with brought in cookies all the time."

Parents and their children may even need to confront the differences about part-time jobs during school vacations. When Julia came home for semester break, her mother assumed she would replenish her bank account by picking up some shifts at the restaurant where she had worked during high school. Julia, however, was looking forward to three and a half weeks of catching up on sleep, meeting up with her high school friends, and reading ahead for her spring semester literature class. She hadn't even considered calling her former boss about working.

"Julia, it's not just that *I* expect you to earn some money," her mother pointed out. "Your financial aid package is based on you contributing toward your college expenses. You can work during your breaks, or you can get a job at school next semester, but you need to be earning some income."

NEW RULES FOR THE MONEY GAME

Over the past few decades, the cost of a college education has increased well beyond the rate of inflation, and families question whether the returns are worth the expense. The answer is, "Generally, yes." College graduates typically earn about $30,000 more per year than their peers who have no postsecondary education or training.[11]

But students have to keep their long-term goals in mind. Spending heavily on school for a degree that doesn't qualify them for a job, or paying high tuition rates for a job that pays a low salary, means they won't get a good return on their investment. In the worst position are the students who take out loans and attend college but never graduate. They qualify only for low-paying jobs, and they have college debt to repay.

Parents also question whether it's really the family's responsibility to pay for their children's education. Shouldn't the students bear the cost of their own education, while parents focus on growing their retirement savings?

Not so long ago, students could work full-time at a summer job, part-time during the school year, and graduate with little or no debt. That is no longer an option. Students who go to school full-time cannot work enough hours to pay room, board, tuition,

---

11. J. R. Abel and R. Deitz, "Despite Rising Costs, College Is Still a Good Investment," *Liberty Street Economics*, June 5, 2019, https://libertystreet economics.newyorkfed.org/2019/06/despite-rising-costs-college-is-still-a-good -investment.html.

fees, books, and other expenses. Those who try to pay as they go, working thirty or more hours a week while taking classes, often end up dropping courses, going to school part-time, and taking longer to finish college. And those who take out high-interest loans to pay for college expenses not covered by grants and low-interest student loans will be repaying huge debts for years after graduation. The better choice is usually to work part-time, take out a low-interest student loan, and finish college within four years. The debt on state and federal loans can be offset by the higher wages that college graduates earn. The bonus is that graduation in four years advances the student into progressively better-paying positions at a younger age.

Where the future of college funding might be headed is unclear. Voices are being raised for such plans as forgiving student debt, providing free college, or guaranteeing two years of postsecondary education for everyone. College funding is a topic of concern for educators, politicians, parents, and students. Many families are finding ways to reduce the cost of college by encouraging their high school juniors and seniors to take "dual enrollment" courses, earning college credit while they complete their high school curriculum.

Options are available for reducing college expenses by serving in the military, participating in ROTC (Reserve Officers' Training Corps), or by majoring and working in a high-need profession. These include public service jobs—typically medical and teaching jobs in rural or low-income areas. Graduates might qualify for debt forgiveness or college loan deductions through public service work or volunteer experiences, including AmeriCorps, Peace Corps, VISTA (Volunteers in Service to America), and Teach For America.

While any number of possibilities could end up reducing the cost of college in the future, the odds are good that some student and family contributions will continue to be expected, and the cost of college will continue to rise. It's not disastrous for students to graduate with some debt. Students who plan for post-college debt generally are more purposeful about their education, and they factor future earnings and loan repayments into their decisions about a major and career choice. The important point is that parents and students should have a solid understanding of anticipated costs, anticipated debts, who will pay for which expenses, and who will repay which loans.

QUICK TIPS FOR STUDENTS

- Like other issues that fall under the heading, "Life is unfair," none of your friends are in the same financial situation as you. Don't try to match your spending to theirs. Don't feel guilty for what you have or ashamed by what you don't have, and don't ever be afraid to say, "I can't afford that."
- Your finances are linked to your family. If you're receiving college loans, your parents' income is figured into the formula until you're twenty-four. That means some of the choices you make will affect their financial situation. Talk to your parents about any decisions you're making that could have an impact on them.
- Hang on to student loan forms, dorm contracts, and credit card agreements, and any statements related to income taxes. Make sure your parents get copies of the statements they need for their income tax.
- Beware of the small print on credit card applications. You may be agreeing to overdraft penalties, an annual fee, an enrollment fee, or a significant increase in interest rates in six months. Make sure you understand the terms and conditions for any credit card you get. Remember: If you don't pay your entire bill

this month, you will pay interest next month. And the company will collect its interest payments before it subtracts anything from the amount you owe.

- Watch for deadlines and payment dates on everything. Filling out a scholarship application a day after the deadline is a waste of time—you're not going to get the scholarship. Credit card payments are based on when your transaction is received at the processing center, not when you mail the check, and probably not the same day you pay online. Late payments mean penalty charges and lower your credit rating. A late payment might also mean a big increase in the interest rate you are charged.

CHAPTER 8

Sex, Drugs, and Drinking Games

The Social Scene

When newly admitted students are asked, "What is your greatest concern about starting college?" they say, "Getting good grades and making friends." When asked what they look forward to the most, they say "freedom" or "independence."

When parents are asked about their greatest concern for their student, they say they're most worried about how their students will use that new freedom and independence, especially in their choices about alcohol, drugs, and sex.

As a parent, you probably have been delivering the lectures for years. Don't drink and drive; drugs are dangerous; sex can lead to pregnancy and disease. Now, when you mention these topics, you get the look that says, "I know what you're going to say, and I really don't need to hear it again."

They're right. They do know what you're going to say. When

it comes to alcohol, drugs, and sex, your children know how you feel. Nevertheless, you will worry, and it doesn't hurt to repeat your values, with positive and supportive messages rather than warnings and threats. In the long run, the best that parents can do is offer guidance and promote strength of character so that their student is making a *choice* each time the issues come up.

Alcohol, drugs, and sex are not one-time decisions. When your first-year student leaves for college, he may assure you he doesn't drink, and he's not going to start. But if his roommate offers to share a six-pack of beer some Saturday evening, he might try just one. Or two. That does not mean he has become a drinker. The next time he's offered a drink, he can still say no. Unless your student loses the *ability* to make that choice, your advice will continue to have an impact.

ALCOHOL: A COLLEGE EPIDEMIC OR KIDS BEING KIDS?

Everyone says it: "College students drink." Turn on any football game on a Saturday afternoon in the fall, and you can pick out the drunken fans in the crowd. So, what are the odds that your child will get through college without excessive drinking? Or maybe you've already accepted the fact that your child will drink at college. After all, by the time kids finish high school, nearly 60 percent have at least tried alcohol.[12]

---

12. J. E. Schulenberg et al., *Monitoring the Future: National Survey Results on Drug Use, 1975–2017*: vol. 2, *College Students and Adults Ages 19–55*, Ann Arbor: Institute for Social Research, University of Michigan, 2018, http://monitoringthefuture.org/pubs.html#monographs (accessed July 15, 2015).

There seem to be three significant factors that serve as strong predictors of a student's drinking or drug use:[13, 14]

- The student's alcohol history during high school
- Parents' use of and attitude toward alcohol and drugs
- Students' perception of drinking levels on campus and among peers

Student's alcohol or drug history during high school: The student who drank excessively in high school is not likely to quit when he arrives at college. That's not to say students are doomed if they partied too much on prom night and that one time after graduation. They might have learned a good lesson when they woke up sick the next morning or had to face disapproving family and friends. A few slip-ups don't confirm a major problem. On the other hand, students who think alcohol and drugs are the key ingredients to having a good time will continue to drink or do drugs in college.

Unfortunately, some students already have substance abuse problems by the time they arrive on campus. The college population represents every level of drinking and drug use, from total abstinence to addiction. Some 10 percent of the college population will become bona fide alcoholics, for the same reasons that

---

13. J. C. Rusby, J. M. Light, R. Crowley, and E. Westling, "Influence of Parent–Youth Relationship, Parental Monitoring, and Parent Substance Use on Adolescent Substance Use Onset," *Journal of Family Psychology* 32, no. 3 (2018): 310–20.

14. C. D. Temmen and L. J. Crockett, "Adolescent Predictors of Social and Coping Drinking Motives in Early Adulthood," *Journal of Adolescence*, 66 (2018): 1–8.

adults become alcoholics. About 20 percent will not drink at all.[15] Students, like their parents, vary widely in their beliefs and behaviors regarding drinking.

Parents' use of and attitude toward alcohol and drugs. Some parents are shocked and disbelieving when they get a call saying that their child has been cited for drinking—not because he was drunk, but because anyone actually cares. "Of course he was drinking. He's a college student, and it's a weekend." Or they explain, "We taught him to drink. He knows his limits. He's fine."

In fact, it's not all that uncommon to see parents on Move-In Day at the start of their student's freshman year hauling in a case of beer for the mini fridge. (Friendly advice: Don't try this. Even if you claim the beer is for you, not your child, the responsibility will fall on your student for having alcohol in the room.)

Students' perception of drinking and drug use on campus and among peers. Even the student who has no particular interest in drinking or marijuana might start, simply because "everyone does it." Peer pressure is powerful. Some colleges have a party school reputation, and drinking is an element of the school's overall image. The beverage of choice or the places where students go to smoke pot might be part of the social environment of the school. Within a single university, students might be heavier drinkers in one particular residence hall or mostly marijuana users on one floor of a dorm. Student athletes and fraternity members have a widespread reputation for binge drinking. That does not mean that all athletes and fraternity members drink. What it does mean is

---

15. American College Health Association, *American College Health Association—National College Health Assessment II: Reference Group Executive Summary*, 2018, Silver Spring, MD: American College Health Association, https://www.acha .org/documents/ncha/NCHA-II_Spring_2018_Reference_Group_Executive _Summary.pdf (accessed June 17, 2019).

that if students think "everyone is doing it," risky behavior feels much more acceptable.

DRINKING IS ILLEGAL, SO MAKE THEM STOP

If alcohol is such a pervasive problem, parents ask, why don't colleges do something about it? Midway through the first semester, DeWayne's father called the dean of students, demanding, "You have to stop the drinking! My son's roommate gets drunk with his friends every weekend, and my kid can't even hang out in his own room because of the mess and the noise. The law says you have to be twenty-one to drink, but the cops just look the other way. What has to happen before you do something about it?"

Colleges are not merely standing by while their underage students drink. Professors do not want hungover, unprepared students in their classrooms. Residence hall staff would really rather not have to clean up after loud, drunk, disorderly, and sick students. Every campus has policies regarding underage drinking. However, most colleges and universities do not routinely search students' rooms, nor will they conduct random checks for illegal substances. Privacy laws prevent staff members from searching students' personal space without cause, and students and their parents would rightly object to inspections of an innocent student's room. Consequently, the students who quietly have a few beers with friends on Friday night probably won't be caught. It's the "noise and nuisance" behavior that alerts staff members, and those cases are confronted.

As "educational institutions," a college might respond to a first alcohol offense, if minor, with a warning, but more serious or repeated violations will result in progressively severe responses, including fines, completion of an alcohol education program, participation in alcohol and drug counseling, cancellation of the student's housing contract, or suspension from college.

HOW WORRIED SHOULD I BE?

Fortunately, it's rare for a college student not to survive a night of heavy partying. That doesn't mean drinking isn't problematic. Drinking has been called the number one behavior problem among college students. It leads to poor grades, sexual assaults, vandalism, wasted time, and wasted money. A few beers every weekend may not seem like a big expense or a major peril, but it adds up.

While it is illegal in the United States to drink until the age of twenty-one,[16] anyone with a credit card and an Internet connection can order a fake identification card and have it delivered by express mail. If students have a slightly older relative who looks like them, or a creative friend with a good printer and a laminating machine, they won't have to wait for a mail delivery to get an ID that just might pass inspection by a sympathetic server who's working for tips. Then again, who needs a fake ID when they know where the keg party is?

The most troublesome trend in college-age drinking is the emphasis on heavy or binge drinking and drinking games. At both the high school and college levels, the goal is not just to drink, but to get drunk as quickly and cheaply as possible. It's one thing to consume a beer or two while watching football on a Saturday afternoon. It's quite another issue when teenagers set out to guzzle a beer in mere seconds, or a six-pack in an hour or less.

---

16. Centers for Disease Control and Prevention, "Alcohol and Public Health Fact Sheet," https://www.cdc.gov/alcohol/fact-sheets/minimum-legal-drinking-age.htm (accessed July 15, 2019).

A Web search for drinking games yields sites featuring dozens of stunts rated by their buzz factor or danger level. The winner is the last person standing. Losers are those who pass out, vomit, or black out. Beer pong and keg stands provide a challenge for the drinker, plus entertainment for observers. Jell-O shots and alco-pops are easy to slide down, providing a quick and painless high. At some schools, a twenty-first birthday might mean standing on the table to drink a pitcher of beer, setting up twenty-one shots to mark the occasion, or searching for free or cheap drinks along a row of campus-area bars.

Students believe that since they're not drinking and driving, they're safe. They're out with their friends, and someone will take care of them. They ask one person to "babysit" the group and make sure no one falls asleep while lying on their back, thinking that will prevent vomit asphyxiation. They choose not to consider the dangers of other types of accidents—fights, falls, hypothermia, and alcohol poisoning. "You're not actually going to die from drinking beer," they tell one another. They know plenty of people who took a twelve-pack to a party and came home safe. "Maybe if you drank a whole bottle of whiskey you'd be in trouble, but you'll get sick from beer and wine before anything really bad happens."

Students don't want to hear warnings about drinking, but they pay attention when they hear statistics that they can apply to themselves. Men listen when they're told that four drinks within an hour will put a 180-pound male over the legal limit for blood alcohol content. Women take notice when they hear that five vodka shots in an hour could mean serious health effects to someone their size, even death.

Half of students who drink report negative consequences as a result of their drinking. Some of the consequences might be temporary, but there are long-term consequences, too. Students who drink heavily have lower grade point averages than nondrinkers.

They're more likely to do something they regret, have unplanned or unwanted sex, or get in trouble with the police.[17]

Recent research shows that the binge drinking that students claim as a harmless break at the end of a busy week can cause serious damage to the brain. Alcohol use by young adults under the age of twenty-one has been shown to damage the memory and learning areas of the brain, and it inhibits the decision-making and reasoning areas—the very parts of the brain students are supposed to be developing during college.

DRUGS: THE LOW-CAL HIGH

Risky behaviors extend to drug use, and students can creatively defend their use by claiming the highs are less messy. "No vomiting, no recycling needed, so it's green!" And, they declare, drugs are less fattening. "All those empty calories in beer? No thanks!"

As with alcohol, the student who never considered drug use might begin because he comes to believe that "it's not really a big deal" when he sees other students casually using drugs. Marijuana is the most readily available drug on college campuses, and in some states legal for those twenty-one and older. As with alcohol, students often arrive as freshmen with experience in buying and using marijuana, and nearly 40 percent of college students use marijuana at least occasionally; about 8 percent are daily users.

Most students—but certainly not all—are cautious of hard drugs such as heroin, cocaine and crack, or opioids. They might be willing to gamble with club drugs and prescription drugs. They think they're playing it safe using the old standbys—beer and liquor—combined with relatively common prescrip-

17. https://www.acha.org/documents/ncha/NCHA-II_Spring_2018_Reference _Group_Executive_Summary.pdf.

tion drugs, such as amphetamines, Benadryl, Ritalin, Adderall, Valium, or Vicodin. "These are legal! What can it hurt to wash down one pill with a drink? You get stoned faster, and the highs last longer." They can even get their health insurance company to pay for the prescription if they fake symptoms, or there may be a kid down the hall willing to sell some pills for quick cash. They don't want to know they are creating potentially lethal cocktails, so they don't pay attention to the labels that warn, "Do not take with alcohol." They choose not to worry about the blackouts or the lingering effects a day later.

The so-called club drugs—tablets or liquids that have found their way into the party scene—pose particular problems when added to alcohol. GHB (gamma hydroxybutyrate) and Rohypnol show up on college campuses across the country and are associated with date rape. With recipes posted online and the finished product available for bargain prices at Mexican spring-break destinations, they are easy to obtain and despairingly effective. Victims rarely recognize the symptoms of the drug, and the traces disappear from the bloodstream within twenty-four hours. By the time a victim begins to understand what happened, it's usually too late to gather evidence.

Because the purity and strength of these drugs are unreliable, their danger is even greater. Taken with alcohol, they can cause coma and death. And, like alcohol, drugs interfere with brain development and can lead to lifelong dependence.

PREVENTION PARTNERSHIPS

Parents might feel more comfortable knowing that their student's college will tell them if their child violates drinking or drug policies, but not all schools will. FERPA, the same federal law that protects student privacy, allows but does not require colleges to notify parents about violations related to alcohol or controlled substances.

Parent notification policies give families a sense of control, but they do not *prevent* problems. Increasingly, colleges are hearing from parents after a serious incident. "Someone is supposed to be looking out for these kids. How could you let us down?"

Even at small, private colleges where staff members do their best to monitor student behavior, it's impossible to keep all students from drinking or doing drugs. At a large university where students have more personal freedom, schools simply cannot supervise every student's every action. Students really are responsible for their own behavior.

A sober student can feel alone sometimes on a college campus. Drinking and partying are common conversation topics on campus, and the students who roar back into the residence hall early Sunday morning attract much more attention and seem more plentiful than their quieter, nondrinking neighbors. Growing numbers of college students, however, are beginning to assert their right to a clean and quiet living environment. Those students who stumble into the dorm, waking their neighbors and throwing up in the bathrooms, are likely to be reported to hall staff and confronted about their disruptive behavior.

The College Party Calendar

Although any student might decide to get high on any given weekend, heavy and dangerous drinking and drug use are more likely at certain times.

• *The first two weeks of classes of every academic term.* Parties are where students meet new friends or celebrate reunions with returning friends. Students haven't established their semester study schedules yet, so it feels like there's plenty of time for fun and socializing.

- *Athletic games, major sports rivalry games* (think Texas-Oklahoma, Michigan–Ohio State, Alabama-Auburn), *and homecoming*. Pre- and post-game partying is a tradition on college campuses. Halloween is a big party night, and the stress of midterms is an easy excuse to use alcohol.
- *Finals.* Anxiety and the intensity of studying combine with unstructured study days and exam days. Celebrating the last final is a ritual at some colleges. Students coming home for long holiday weekends or semester breaks frequently drink heavily when they get together with their high school friends.
- *Midwinter weekends and winter or spring celebrations.* In cold-weather climates, drinking may be the winter pastime. Mardi Gras and St. Patrick's Day provide excuses for dressing up and throwing a party. Campus spring-fling festivals often coincide with the conclusion of midterm exams.
- *Spring break.* Escapes to warm locations bring students together from all around the country. The partying is legendary.
- *The end of the academic year.* Students plan gatherings with friends before leaving for the summer. Seniors, old enough to drink legally, are beginning the graduation festivities at the same time they're facing the uncertainty of starting a new job, moving to a new location, and facing the postcollege debts. "This is the end of an era," they say, and the nostalgia they're suffering includes a last chance for college partying.

PARENTS CAN HELP

An often-overlooked protective factor against drinking and drug use involves the continuing influence of parents. Research shows that students who abstain from drinking often do so because their parents discuss alcohol use and its consequences with them. Parents' conversations about alcohol and drugs make a difference by reducing the impact of peer pressure. A young adult's relationship with her parents continues to play a major protective role in promoting smart choices throughout college. It's helpful, then, for parents to continue discussing expectations related to alcohol and drug use.

During the crucial early weeks of the first semester, parents can do a number of things to stay involved:

- Talk with their student about the dangers of harmful and underage college drinking—such as the penalties for underage drinking, and how alcohol use can lead to sexual and other violence, as well as academic failure and other adverse consequences.
- Reach out periodically and keep the lines of communication open, while staying alert for possible alcohol-related problems.
- Remind your student to feel free to stay in touch, share information about their daily activities, and ask for help if needed.
- Learn about the school's alcohol prevention and emergency intervention efforts.
- Make sure your student knows the signs of alcohol overdose or an alcohol-related problem, and how to help their friends if they need to.

Parents can reinforce the message that all college students do not take drugs or drink to excess. And they can call their student on the excuses: "You should be able to have fun without drugs and alcohol." "Even if you think it's a stupid law, it's still the law. Don't ask me to pay the fine or bail you out if you're arrested."

LET'S TALK ABOUT S-E-X

Most of us find it easiest to avoid thinking or talking about either our parents' or our children's sex lives. Although many students avoid discussing sex with their parents, sex is one of the paramount issues of the college years, and they are thinking about it. A lot. Parents might not ever know when their student has his or her first sexual experience, but the hope is that the first time is not "something that just happened."

Hattie hadn't dated much in high school, but she met her first real boyfriend in college. When she went home for spring break, she mentioned to her mother, Joan, that she needed a dress for her boyfriend's fraternity formal. The dance was off campus, at a hotel ballroom downtown. "I don't want you to worry, Mom, but just so you know, we're staying at the hotel after the dance. We're not doing anything wrong—no sex or anything. Gabe just turned twenty-one, so it's legal for him to drink, and he doesn't want to drive back to campus. It's not like he'll get totally trashed, but we want to be safe. It's not a big thing."

Although Joan's first instinct was to forbid her daughter to even return to school, she took a deep breath and said, "Hattie, let's be realistic. It sounds like you're saying you're going to stay in a hotel room with a young man you like a lot. I would think there's at least a chance you'll have sex. Maybe you could come up with a specific plan for *not* having sex. Like getting a separate room for yourself. Or make sure you're both ready if you're going to sleep together. Please don't put yourself in a situation where you end up going farther than you want to or plan to. I'd just like you to talk about this with him so you both know what the evening is about, and so you won't have any regrets later."

As Hattie stormed off, fuming that her mother didn't trust her, Joan worried that she had just given her daughter permission to have sex with her boyfriend. A few hours later, though, Hattie came back and acknowledged that her mother was right. "I don't know if you want to hear this, Mom, but Gabe is the nicest guy I've ever met, and I like him a lot. We haven't had sex yet, but the truth is, a couple of weeks ago I picked up a package of condoms, and I've had them with me in case things went that far. You're right—I should talk to him about it, and if it's going to happen the night of the dance, I would rather know that it's what we both want."

Hattie was fortunate that her mother was willing to confront the issue. For too many students, sex is unplanned or unwanted, or it's simply not thought through. And that can lead to regrets, resentment, or unwillingness to take responsibility.

WHEN GOOD TIMES GO BAD

Sometimes students don't have the opportunity to make their own choices. Between 20 and 25 percent of women will be raped or sexually assaulted during college. About 15 percent of college men are victims of forced sex.[18] In the vast majority of cases, the assailant is a friend, classmate, or acquaintance. Students believe they're safe, spending time with a friend, and they're unprepared when the situation becomes sexual. Most of these assaults take place in the victim's own residence, leaving no place to escape to.

Because victims often know their assailant, their reactions

---

18. National Sexual Violence Resource Center, "Campus Sexual Assault," https://www.nsvrc.org/node/4737 (accessed August 23, 2019).

are complicated. They blame themselves, thinking, "I must have somehow signaled that it was okay." They experience guilt, wondering if they could have done something to stop or prevent the attack. They're confused about whether it was really rape, believing that since they brought the person into the room, or they went somewhere together willingly, no one would consider it an assault. They even wonder if it actually happened, since, "He's always been such a nice guy. Everyone likes him."

Acquaintance or date rape is often minimized as "not a real rape." The victim decides not to make a report, fearing either that her assailant will retaliate or, by reporting the assault, that she may ruin his reputation or her own. She concludes that no one will believe her, knowing that "it's my word against his." Men who are assaulted bear a different kind of shame and humiliation, feeling they've lost their masculinity. "Why couldn't I stop this? I should have fought back. Why didn't I?" If the student who was assaulted is gay, lesbian, bisexual, or transgender, there might be additional concerns about being "outed" if the assault is reported.

The trauma of acquaintance rape is often compounded by continuing to see the attacker around campus or in the classroom. If the attacker is acting normally, while the victim is churning inside with fear and shame, unable even to talk about the assault, grades and other personal relationships suffer.

Students especially dread telling their parents about an acquaintance rape. They want their parents to believe they are responsible and safe. If they think they could have handled things differently, they worry that their parents will have the same doubts. Students also know that their rape will affect their parents. They don't want to cause them pain or sadness.

In many cases, by withholding the information from their parents, students are protecting themselves from fully acknowledging what happened. If it wasn't "real," maybe they don't have to deal with it. Once they tell the story, they have to face the situation squarely.

Jenna always had a close relationship with her parents. "I never understood my friends who wouldn't tell their parents about the parties they went to or the boys they dated. I told my parents everything!" But when she was sexually assaulted in her residence hall early in her sophomore year, she did not tell her family.

It was Jenna's mother, Connie, who finally figured it out. "Looking back, I should have known right away," Connie recalled. "She called and asked to come home one weekend unexpectedly, and she seemed so exhausted. She asked me to do her laundry and wash her sheets, and she went up to her room and slept. I thought maybe she was just tired—she had some demanding classes that semester. When it was time to go back to school, she was so sad. Always before, she had been happy to get back to her dorm. She was almost clingy toward her dad and me, and it just wasn't like her."

As the year progressed, Jenna seemed anxious. She would call home and cry, complaining about noises outside her room or boys who seemed "too friendly." Her grades dropped significantly. At one point, Jenna mentioned to her mother that she didn't drink anymore because once, after she had been at a party, she fell asleep and didn't wake up until the next afternoon. When she finally did wake up, she couldn't remember anything about the night before.

Toward the end of the second semester, Connie happened to read an article about a college student who had been given a date-rape drug. According to the story, some of the woman's sorority sisters noticed that she was disoriented and sleepy after only one drink. When she fell asleep and her friends couldn't wake her, they called an ambulance. The words on the page blurred as Connie began to recognize that her daughter had exhibited many of the same symptoms the article described—confusion, exhaustion, memory lapse, and lingering depression. Had Jenna been drugged and raped?

Connie searched for the orientation materials from Jenna's freshman year and found a phone number for the campus program that served victims of rape and assault. The director of the program suggested that she could just mention to Jenna that there are peer counselors on campus who are trained to work with students who have been assaulted. If Jenna wasn't yet ready to deal with the situation, she might not be able to discuss it yet. If she was ready, she might need only a gentle nudge.

During their next phone conversation, Connie told Jenna, "I was looking through some information I picked up when you started college, and it reminded me there are peer counselors—students your age—who can talk about rape and sexual assault. Apparently they have drop-in hours, so people can go in anytime and talk to them. It sounds like a good program if you ever know of anyone who needs it."

Jenna didn't ask why her mother was giving her the information. She simply said she would look into it. That week she went to the office, and a few weeks later she went home and told her parents what had happened to her.

Parents' reaction to their child's assault is intense. It feels like an assault on you. Jenna's father was furious, and he was ready to pound on the young man's door and bodily remove him from the college. Jenna's mother was more concerned with taking care of her daughter. She encouraged Jenna to take as much time as she needed and to follow the advice of her peer counselor. The counselor arranged for Jenna to move to a different residence hall, where she would no longer have to see where her assault occurred. She also helped Jenna file a petition through the registrar's office to have her grades for fall semester changed from letter grades to "pass." The support of her family, including both the caregiving from her mother and the fierce loyalty of her father, gave Jenna the courage to work through the recovery process.

In Case of Rape: How a Parent Can Help

- First and foremost, listen and believe your child. Talking about sexual assault is a critical step toward recovery, but it is difficult for both the victim/survivor and for the listener.
- Make sure that "first steps" are taken. Be certain that your child is no longer in danger. If the assault was recent, encourage your child to seek medical attention and support. It's important that evidence is gathered, pregnancy prevention is provided, and sexually transmitted infections are addressed. Decisions about filing charges do not have to be made immediately.
- Many colleges and universities have sexual assault support programs, and services are also available in most communities. You can encourage your child to seek help, but avoid being overly protective or assuming a controlling role. You cannot fix this; there is work to be done, but doing that work is part of the healing process for the victim/survivor. The assault took away your child's power, and it's important for a victim/survivor to assume self-control again and to know that the family supports her or his decisions.
- Recognize and respect your own feelings of anger and helplessness. You can find information for yourself by checking the library or online, or talk to someone at a local rape counseling program. You can also contact the Rape, Abuse and Incest National Network (RAINN) at rainn.org.
- It is not your role to retaliate. Your child knows the situation best. In some cases, a victim may not be able or ready

to confront or even blame the assailant; don't put your
child in the situation of defending the attacker to you.

CAN THEY TAKE CARE OF THEMSELVES?

College students, as a population, are bright, inquisitive adults
who have every resource available to make wise choices. They
arrive at college having heard the message that abstinence is
the only sure method of birth control, and they know there are
plenty of options to prevent pregnancy as well as sexually transmitted infections. How could any student possibly end up with
an unwanted pregnancy or a venereal disease?

All the sex education in the world, however, doesn't alter
the fact that college-aged men and women are biologically programmed to desire intimacy, and they are at a prime age for being
sexual. Depending on the culture of the school or your child's
group of friends, student attitudes toward sex may seem alarm-
ingly impersonal or even cavalier.

When Rachel walked through her daughter's residence hall
lobby on Move-In Day, she noticed a basket of condoms on an
information table. While her daughter was filling out forms,
Rachel softly asked the student staffing the table, "Couldn't you
just put those condoms out of sight until the parents are gone?
We really don't need to see that." Later she asked the hall director, "How can I tell my daughter it's okay *not* to have sex when
you have condoms right there, the first thing she sees on Move-
In Day? How do I get her to believe that not all college students
are having sex all the time?"

While students seem to know the basic facts about sexually
transmitted diseases and infections (STDs and STIs), many don't
think they're at risk. As long as they're hooking up with good,
smart college students like themselves, they are confident they

will be fine. Condoms will protect them from pregnancy and any weird diseases that might be lurking in their partner's distant past. The human papillomavirus (HPV) vaccine will keep them safe from genital warts and maybe cancer sometime down the line. They don't think about the HPV strains that the vaccine doesn't affect, and they don't realize that condoms do not protect them from some of the most common STIs. Even more disturbing, although college students have easy access to condoms and know they offer protection, only about half of students reported using a condom the last time they had sex.[19] They may know how to be safe, but they don't necessarily use that knowledge.

Some parents would prefer that the message to college students be a one-word statement: wait. The mother of an incoming freshman criticized the orientation program at her son's college because a segment of the program included skits about sexuality, pregnancy, and sexually transmitted diseases. "Don't talk about these things, and they won't think sex is an option," she declared.

Many students do abstain. Over the course of a year, three-fourths of college students reported they had sex with no one or with just one partner.[20] Nevertheless, whether or not universities (and parents) address intimacy issues, sex will be on the minds of students. The good news is, you still have some influence. Let your student know your expectations and continue to encourage safe choices. And keep talking. Then, if the time comes when

---

19. American College Health Association–National College Health Assessment II: Reference Group Executive Summary, 2018, Silver Spring, MD: American College Health Association, https://www.acha.org/documents /ncha/NCHA-II_Fall_2018_Reference_Group_Executive_Summary.pdf.

20. Ibid.

your child needs to tell you about a sex-related issue, it will be easier for both of you.

It's not unusual for students to struggle with telling their parents if they are planning to move in with an intimate partner, taking a trip with a boyfriend or girlfriend, or if there's a pregnancy, sexually transmitted disease, or a dysfunction. They may tell you if they are gay, but for most students who are gay, lesbian, bisexual, transgender, or questioning their sexual identity, telling family members is the hardest part of coming out.

Although most students at least begin to identify their sexual orientation in high school or earlier, some will not recognize or accept their gender identity until their college years. On campus, students have a chance to examine their identity in a new setting. They may come to realize that the feelings they have wondered about or hidden for years are part of who they authentically are.

Most colleges and universities have support groups for gay, lesbian, bisexual, and transgender students. Finding a place to ask questions and get answers helps students realize they're not alone. Coming out feels as if a burden has been lifted, but it can bring a few new problems. How will friends and family react?

When Christopher told his parents he was gay, his mother felt almost as much relief as he did. She had seen how unhappy he often seemed, and she had sometimes wondered if he might be gay. She also saw that a cloud had lifted with his coming out. His father, on the other hand, was miserable. He went through every cliché. "You just haven't met the right girl. It will pass." "Is this one of those college things? You'll change your mind when you get out in the real world." "Maybe I should have done more with you when you were growing up."

Still, he also saw that his son was becoming more confident and content. "I'm not exactly happy about this," he told his wife. "I can't help but hope that he'll decide he's not gay, but maybe that's my problem, not his. Chris really is a great kid, and what

I want most for him is to be happy. It does seem like a load has been lifted from his shoulders these days."

Whether the subject is pregnancy, a sexually transmitted disease, or sexual identity, students rehearse the conversation many times before their parents hear the words, "Mom, Dad, I need to tell you something." Even if they've previously talked to a doctor, a counselor, or a friend, now that they're telling their parents, they are beginning to accept and adjust to their situation.

What your student tells you may conflict with everything you believe and everything you have hoped for for your child. You may be hearing something that forces you to revise how you have always looked at your son or daughter. Any objections you voice, however, will not change what your student is telling you. Any suggestions you make will not undo the situation. Your child needs you now, more than ever. Practice these steps in advance so that you're ready if you ever face a tough conversation:

- Listen.
- Say, "Thank you for telling me."
- Ask how your child is feeling; ask what you can do to be helpful.
- Say, "I love you." Then be quiet again in case there's more listening you need to do.

STALKING AND CYBERSTALKING

Harassment and stalking have long been problems on college campuses, but the wonders of technology continue to create new forms of bullying. Schools require students to have campus email accounts, and they collect cell phone numbers for sending automated texts and phone messages. And since this information is readily available in campus directories, those accounts can then be misused for electronic stalking. Text messaging and social media mean harassment can show up on a screen or phone anytime. And what might seem like innocent, online flirting or teasing to the sender of a message may feel like intimidation to the recipient.

A freshman noticed an attractive girl one afternoon at a coffee shop and overheard her friend call her Celeste. Before he could gather his nerve to talk to her, he watched the girl go out the door and cross the street. That evening, still thinking about the "cute coffee shop girl," he checked the school's online directory for anyone named Celeste. It didn't take long to narrow down his search to the Celeste who lived in West Hall, right across the street from the coffee shop. A search on social media sites revealed photos confirming he had found the right girl. He sent an email to her university account, saying he had seen her at the coffee shop at 4:00 p.m. and noticed she was wearing a Film Club sweatshirt. "I'll join the Film Club if it means hanging out with you. Let's meet. Coffee shop across the street from your dorm, 4:00 p.m. tomorrow?" he wrote.

When she didn't show up the next afternoon, he sent a text message using the cell phone number listed in the college directory. "I really want to meet you. West Hall lobby 2nite @8."

To Celeste, the messages felt threatening. Someone she didn't know was describing her clothes and her movements. He knew her email address and phone number, and he knew where she lived. Her residence adviser encouraged her to call the campus police, who checked the boy's email address, found his student ID photo, and sent an officer to wait for him in the residence hall lobby that evening. "You've crossed a line," the officer told him. "I talked to the person who reported you, and we agreed that you might not understand how it would feel to get a message like this. I'm just giving you a warning here, but don't use the campus directory again to track down people who don't know you. And I have a message for you from the girl: do not contact her again."

Cyberstalking is not always an innocent misunderstanding. Electronic harassment is a weapon in the arsenal of spurned boyfriends and girlfriends. It's no longer rare for a student, after a breakup, to be persistently stalked or discover that an intimate photo shared during a relationship has been sent to everyone the couple knows.

A student's first instinct might be to delete hurtful messages and hope nothing ever shows up again, but students should save the message and contact a campus authority or the police. If the harassment or stalking is sent through a campus account, the school's technology office should also be notified. The computer services staff will do their best to track messages back to the source. Every college should have a policy addressing stalking and electronic harassment. To stop the harassment, students can block cell phone numbers and email addresses, change their own email ID and password, and use privacy settings on social media and campus directories.

QUICK TIPS FOR STUDENTS
Take Care of Yourself

- Safety first. When you're preparing for a date or a party, know how you can safely get home on your own if you need to. Have your phone charged and with you. Have a trusted ride-share app on your phone and enough money for a cab if that's your best option.
- Drink responsibly. The vast majority of sexual assaults and violence among college students follows drinking by one or both individuals. Be aware of how alcohol affects you. If drinking makes you more aggressive,

you could be in danger of harming someone. Being drunk is not an excuse for committing sexual assault.

- Trust your instincts. If you find yourself in a situation where something feels wrong or you feel unsafe, look for a way to take control of the situation—move closer to other people or seek a safe way to get home.

- Don't ignore sudden feelings of mistrust just because you have known someone for a long time. You can't always tell what a person is like based on past behaviors.

- Never leave a drink unattended or accept a drink that you did not see poured. Date-rape drugs can leave you unable to protect yourself, or even know what's happening to you.

- Take assertiveness training and self-defense classes. If you become frightened, do your best to be forceful. Speak loudly and firmly or yell.

- If you are sexually assaulted, go to a clinic or emergency room as soon as you can. You can decide later whether or not to press charges, but you need to receive medical attention and caring support as soon as possible.

Take Care of Your Friends
- At parties or bars, keep your friends in sight. Watch out for each other, and check in from time to time to make sure you're all comfortable with how things are going.

- If you notice someone getting out of control—drinking too much, arguing, or behaving inappropriately—do what you can to distract the person or calm things down. Don't put yourself in danger, but don't ignore a potentially harmful situation. Recruit others to develop a plan and to help intervene if necessary.

- Don't let your friends do something stupid, and never ask them to cover for your bad behavior. A bystander can be charged with complicity if they know about an assault and fail to intervene. This includes sexual assault. Complicity can mean a steep fine or jail time.

CHAPTER 9

Study Snacks and All-Nighters

Health and Wellness

A dining service director polled students to find out which breakfast cereals to stock in the campus cafeteria. The top choices: Special K with Red Berries, Cinnamon Crunch, Lucky Charms, and Cracklin' Oat Bran.

Any college freshman can tell you about healthy eating. They know what they should eat, and they know how poor nutrition affects their health. Nevertheless, sugar and caffeine dominate the healthy choices in their daily diet. Students also know the theoretical benefits of a good night's rest and regular exercise, but sleep and daily workouts are among the casualties when a paper is due or something comes up that sounds like more fun.

A steady diet of soda, candy, and chips provides quick energy, but it doesn't contribute nourishment or stamina for the long haul. Students might manage to stay up long into the night talking with friends or cramming for a quiz, but they make up for the late hours by dozing off during lectures or searching out a secluded spot in the library for a nap between classes. With each passing week, they become more susceptible to any illnesses that might be lurking around campus.

HEALTHY CHOICES

As parents look over the list of their child's college dining plan options, they're swayed by the most extensive meal choice. They want their child to eat three meals a day, and the full meal plan or an "unlimited" option seems the most economical on a per-meal breakdown. Then before second semester starts, their child mentions that she might as well cut back to the fourteen-meals-per-week plan. She says she would be saving money; her parents are convinced she'll starve.

Breakfast may be the most important meal of the day, but on a college campus, it's the least popular. Few college students can be classified as "morning people." They prefer to sleep as late as possible before dashing off to class. Those with 8:00 a.m. classes don't have time for breakfast; those who sleep past 9:00 plan for an early lunch to cover two meals at one sitting. At best, breakfast becomes little more than a quick stop to grab a banana, bagel, and a Coke. If you're hoping to ensure that your student has a decent start to the day, you might make a better invest-ment by buying or renting a dorm-size refrigerator and suggest-ing your child shop regularly for milk, juice, and cereal.

There is logic in choosing the two-meals-per-day plan, but students still protest that they can't possibly eat in the dining center that often. "On Mondays and Wednesdays, I'm in class until 1:00 p.m., and all the good stuff is gone by the time I get there." "Sometimes I need a break from cafeteria food."

College dietitians might have the most important—and least appreciated—jobs on campus. "Choice" has become the cafete-ria watchword, and chefs strive for a creative variety of options. Salad bars with dozens of choices are standard, and most din-ing centers have cereal, sandwich, soup, and pasta bars, as well as made-to-order stir-fry. Burgers, chicken patties, and fries are always on the lunch and dinner menus. Vegetarians and vegans will find entrées that fit their dietary demands, or at least they should be able to build a meal around the vegetables, pasta, salad, and bread options. Increasingly, dining centers are offering ethnic imperatives, such as side dishes of rice and tortillas at every meal.

At some schools, students can use their dining dollars at on-campus restaurants, which might include popular fast-food chains. Vending machines are stocked with sweet, savory, and healthy snacks for students whose hunger hits at night. Those snacks might not be selections that make parents feel better about their child's diet, but they are popular supplements among students.

Still, students complain. Ethan's mother had dismissed his occasional grumbling about the food until one night, in the middle of the week, he showed up at home just as she was sitting down for dinner. "I got a ride home so I could have some real food for a change. What have you got? I need a break from the dining center. I swear, the vegetables are mushy, the meat is gray, and they even manage to mess up the orange juice."

Food was a factor Ethan's mother had been especially concerned about before her son started college. Ethan was one of those high school students who ate steadily from the time they got home in the afternoon until they went to bed. She had called the dining center to be sure he could have second servings and a range of choices at each meal. The food service director invited her to come for a meal the next time she was on campus, and she had taken him up on the offer. She was impressed with what she saw on her visit, and Ethan's complaints didn't make sense based on what she had seen.

Sometimes, when students complain to their parents about food, there are other, undisclosed issues. In Ethan's case, the real motive was that he wanted to move out of the residence hall. He had an invitation from his lab partner to sublet the second bedroom of an apartment near campus, but he knew his mother would object. She had already told him she wanted him to stay in the dorm another year. He also knew, though, that he could gain her sympathy by claiming the food was inedible.

Food gets the blame when students want to transfer to a school closer to a boyfriend or girlfriend, when they want to join a fraternity or sorority, or when they're having roommate problems and simply don't want to stay where they are. It's also the pretext when they don't have friends to eat with, and they just cannot bear sitting alone again.

Using food as an excuse is a brilliant means of persuasion. What parent can ignore a fundamental requirement of life? A kid has to eat. If a student were to complain about the roommate, parents would suggest, "Talk it over. Ask the hall director to help. Maybe it's partly your fault?" But few parents will tell their students to tough it out when they hear they're not eating. What's more, it's almost a form of flattery—your child likes family meals, and nothing else can compare.

Admittedly, dishes prepared for a college dining center will not taste like home cooking. Because of the range of food sensitivities and allergies among the college population, the recipes are generally not seasoned like home cooking. The student who is accustomed to having butter slathered on fresh, al dente vegetables will probably find that steam-table corn and peas are bland. At the end of most serving lines, though, a spice bar provides salt, pepper, herbs, hot sauce, salsa, and the old standbys, ketchup, mustard, and mayonnaise.

Complaints about the food provide students with a social bond. They connect with one another through shared suffering, and caustic remarks about "mystery meat" or "spaghetti soup" provide easy conversation starters and sometimes lead to a group trip downtown for pizza or dessert.

Sometimes, though, the food genuinely *is* bad, and students' complaints are the impetus for improvement. An unskilled food service director may be revealed only if students speak out.

How do you determine if the problem is serious, or if it might be a veiled effort to move out of the dorm? Parents can ask about the options that are typically provided. Do they have salad and pasta bars? Is there at least one dish that's palatable at each meal? If a student takes an entrée and doesn't like it, can she go back for something else? If your student has dietary restrictions, has he talked to the dietitian about special meals or asked for guidance in selecting foods that fit his requirements?

If you live close enough or are visiting campus, find out if you can have a meal with your student. Meal plans often include a few guest passes, so a meal for you might already be paid for. If not, ask if family members can pay to go through the cafeteria line.

Although in most cases, the food really is pretty good, anyone who has eaten in a college dining center understands that the prospect of pulling every meal, every day from a cafeteria line can wear on you. Students are expected to choose from dozens of options—which students demand—but the noise of hundreds of young adults talking, flatware clinking against plates, hamburgers sizzling, and the occasional breaking glass or dropped tray adds up to a constant din. Each meal becomes sensory overload. Every now and then, a student needs the break of a solitary meal while watching a video in his room, or a quiet restaurant in off-peak hours with a good friend and quiet conversation. If you can't add a little cash to the budget for extra meals from time to time, encourage your student to occasionally request the cafeteria's brown bag, takeaway lunch just to provide a break from the routine.

ALL WORK AND NO PLAY

Sometimes even students who eat three healthy meals a day can go through a physical decline. We've all heard of the "freshman fifteen," those extra pounds that students pile on by opting for spaghetti and breadsticks for every meal, 400-calorie caramel macchiatos between classes, and an eight-ounce bag of cheese curls before bed. It's a college ritual to go out for chicken wings on Sunday night, and it's part of the daily routine to gather in the lounge for sodas and popcorn a couple of times a day. It may seem like walking to class while carrying a twenty-pound backpack would substitute for a gym workout, but students can quickly get out of shape.

Young adults are fully aware that exercise improves overall health, reduces stress, and helps prevent weight gain, but workouts become a luxury when time is tight. Athletes who are no longer competing in sports don't have a daily exercise routine. Those who have never previously given much attention to working out might not feel much desire to start.

If exercise is ever to become a lifelong regimen, the college years are key. Health habits picked up during college last into adulthood. Students will never again have quite as many recreational options. Campuses provide a range of athletic facilities, intramural teams, and state-of-the-art gym equipment at no charge or for a bargain-rate fee. Students can try sports they've only seen on TV or read about in books. Those who dreaded the required volleyball games in middle school gym class might find their niche in a college fencing club. Earning course credit for lacrosse, snorkeling, or horseback riding can provide a new outlook on exercise. Maybe a class in Latin dance or bowling will make Monday mornings more interesting and teach useful talents for Friday night entertainment.

As with other lifestyle issues, parents can't force their students to exercise, but you can point out the recreation center's features, ask what sounds interesting, and encourage participation. Your own behavior is also influential. When you exercise regularly, your student gets a message about the importance of making healthy activities part of a daily schedule. You don't need to dwell on the number of steps you chalk up every day or how many calories you burn, but you can talk about what you saw during your morning walk or mention that you stopped at the gym on the way home from work. You also can plan hikes and bicycle tours into your visits to campus or schedule family time on the community ski slope during winter break.

WHEN THE FLU BUG BITES

It's a horrible feeling to have your child call home and say, "I'm sick." Even if she only has a cold and you know she'll be fine with a bit of rest, you will feel helpless and anxious.

Students share germs in all kinds of creative ways—curling up on the floor with a roommate's pillow, using a friend's earbuds to listen to a new tune, and picking the pepperoni off someone's slice of pizza. One junior swears that she and all her friends contracted pink eye by playing with her roommate's kitten. You can trust that every student will come down with the flu or at least have a nasty headache at some point during the year.

You know your child, and you know if he tends to overdramatize when he's sick, or if he's likely to complain only if he is in serious pain. When you hear your child asking for help or sympathy, trust your past experiences and rely on your long-standing routines, at least to the extent that you can through distance communication. A phone or video diagnosis doesn't permit you to confirm with a hand on the forehead just how sick your child is, and your student may not be able to relay satisfactory answers when you ask, "Do you feel like you have a fever? Are you flushed?"

When students call to tell you they're sick, they are looking for the pampering they received as a child. They want to hear the advice they know you will provide: go to bed, drink lots of juice, take a pain reliever, and heat up a cup of chicken soup. They would like you to tell them how long it will be before they feel better. Just hearing the concern in your voice serves as a virtual hug.

Unfortunately, many students don't want to even acknowledge an illness. Students who are trying to establish independence believe that any health problem is a sign that they can't take care of themselves after all. One young man suffered for a week with an ingrown toenail, treating it with a topical ointment and limping to and from classes. He went to the health service only when his toe swelled so much he could no longer get his shoe on. A young woman with a rash on her buttocks was too embarrassed to tell anyone or make a clinic appointment. "It will clear up," she thought. After two weeks of itching, she had to admit that it was getting worse. She finally called her mother, only to receive the obvious advice. "You need to see a doctor."

When students are ill and away from home, the last thing they need is the stress of figuring out how to make a medical appointment and learning to deal with health insurance. There are some things you can do before your child leaves for college:

- Be sure that you and your student know what services are available on campus and when to seek help off campus. Even schools with a health service on campus might require students to go to a local clinic or hospital for urgent care or weekend appointments.

- Give your student an insurance card with coverage information and a company phone number. If copayments are required at the time of service, be sure your student has emergency funds or payment information to be used for that purpose.
- Students on their parents' health insurance must know how to make a claim. Many health insurance plans are tied to specific clinics or a provider area; coverage might be different when the student is away from home, and a doctor's appointment may require preapproval. In some cases, copayments are different for care outside the coverage area. Students must know if they're required to contact the insurance company before seeking care.
- Explain your family prescription plan, including how to obtain new prescriptions and refills.
- If your child uses eyeglasses or contact lenses, be sure he has a copy of the most recent prescription.
- Talk about dental coverage; for a student, a chipped tooth or broken filling is a devastating problem. If you have emergency dental coverage, let your student know what it covers and how to use it.
- Be sure your student understands that if he makes a claim on your insurance, you will receive notice of that claim. Discuss whether you will need to know what the treatment was for.

PREDICTING PROBLEMS

Cold and flu season hits campus about the time students are preparing for midterm exams. If shorter days and falling temperatures are not enough to dim the excitement of first-year students, upcoming tests are a reminder that college work is wearing them down. Students search for the perfect recipe to help them stay awake, and in a show of camaraderie, upperclassmen pass along their recommendations to new students: "Mountain Dew has more caffeine than any other beverage in the soda machine downstairs, but energy drinks are available at the convenience store across the street. The purpose of study snacks is to keep you alert," they advise. "Try combining equal parts of peanuts, raisins, and chocolate-covered coffee beans."

As immune systems are pushed to the limit, students start coming down with any passing illness. Then they postpone treatment "until I have time." Homework deadlines and tests are a much higher priority than a cough or an ache. By the time they can work a clinic call into their schedule, they're miserable and hoping for an immediate appointment and a quick fix.

Freshmen are especially determined to tough it out, no matter how miserable they may be. The first-year student who comes down with the flu a couple of months into the first semester will drag herself to all her classes, even if she coughs and wheezes throughout the lecture. After working so hard to get into college, waiting so long to arrive on campus, and dreaming so much of what college would be, it's unfathomable to think she could possibly be sick. That wasn't in any picture she had of college.

Students are likely to get sick just after they meet the deadline for a major project. Any class that includes public speaking will raise stress levels and lower endurance. Final exam week takes a lot out of students, and a bad cold develops just after they come home for the holidays or for the summer. Within a few weeks after a student moves into his first apartment, he might end up on the edge of malnourishment—the reality of meal preparation is harder than it seemed. And as the senior faces decisions about graduate school or job hunting, anxiety can cause stomach pain or headaches.

Parents feel torn between the desire to honor their children's desire for independence and the need to protect their health. In most cases, the best parents can do is support their students as they grow increasingly self-reliant. Although colleges provide forms for release of financial and academic information to family members, those forms don't include access to health records. Unless the student is willing to sign a form releasing health information, parents will not have access to their son's or daughter's medical records. And even then, you may have to know when to ask for those records. A physician or a psychologist might encourage your child to *tell* you about a health condition, but she might not be calling about the diagnosis and treatment options.

COLLEGE ILLNESS: THE LIKELY SUSPECTS

It's difficult to entrust your child's well-being to health professionals you've never met, but campus health service staff are particularly knowledgeable about the problems that college-aged students are susceptible to. Some mental and physical conditions are especially associated with young adults, and the nurses, doctors, and other clinic staff know what to look for. The short list includes mononucleosis, meningitis, eating disorders, and several mental health conditions, including anxiety and depression. The onset of asthma, diabetes, schizophrenia, and other disorders can show up in this age group as well.

Mononucleosis: Soon after the start of classes every fall, college health professionals watch for cases of mono. First-year students are especially likely to downplay the early symptoms. Adjustment to college, change in diet, and lack of sleep all contribute to weakening the immune system and increasing the risk of illness. Students who ignore the early symptoms, believing "it's just a cold," end up exhausted and dehydrated, barely able to make it to the clinic for an appointment.

Meningitis: The first thing to keep in mind about meningitis is that incidence rates are low. There are both viral and bacterial varieties, and the most serious variety, bacterial meningitis, is rare. Meningitis infects the membrane surrounding the brain and spinal cord. Viral meningitis is painful and often requires hospitalization, but it's much less likely than the bacterial variety to cause serious consequences. Bacterial meningitis can result in severe long-term health problems or even death.

Students who live in residence halls or fraternity and sorority houses—places where there are close quarters, a population with stressed immune systems, and the tendency to overlook simple sanitation—are in an environment that bacterial meningitis prefers. The bacteria spread when students share a soda or a kiss, or through contamination from coughs and sneezes. Its early symptoms mimic the flu or colds: headache, fever, sensitivity to light, sore throat, and nausea. One of the danger signs is a stiff neck and inability to bend the chin down to touch the upper chest. Because meningitis can progress rapidly, it requires a quick diagnosis and treatment.

Vaccines are available to protect against bacterial meningitis. Some colleges and universities require students to be vaccinated. If your student's college does not require the vaccine, talk to your physician about immunization.

Eating disorders: Eating disorders are not confined to first-year students, but they may be exacerbated by the initial stress of leaving home. The complications of so many life changes at once can send students looking either for the comfort of food or for something they can control. Either way, food becomes the focus. When we think of eating disorders, we commonly think of anorexia and bulimia and their effects on women. These are the most common disorders, but not the only ones, and college men are also affected by eating disorders.

Those who struggle with anorexia or bulimia are so deeply

preoccupied by food, diet, and body image that there is no room in their thoughts to acknowledge the self-harm they're causing. Every day is centered around counting calories consumed, estimating calories burned, stepping on the scales to see if they're making progress, and enduring immense guilt for any slip-ups. Meanwhile, they probably are being flattered by their peers for their slender figure.

Students who experienced eating disorders during high school are especially at risk when they begin college, but anyone with an obsession about food may develop an eating disorder. In some cases, women in residence halls and sororities have taken bingeing and purging to the level of group activity. They might spend an evening gorging on snacks, then support one another as they justify the logic of getting rid of all those calories.

Eating disorders almost always require some form of intervention and counseling, but family and friends face a daunting task when they try to help. These disorders are complex. Until victims want to change, they will find ways to continue their behavior. As a parent, you can point out what you are seeing, express your concern, and talk about options for seeking help. Recovery requires professional assistance.

For information about eating disorders, the family's role, and where to find assistance, check the National Eating Disorders Association (NEDA) website: https://www.nationaleatingdisor ders.org/.

Depression: Clinical depression is often first diagnosed during the late teens and early twenties, but to complicate matters, college students are living a lifestyle that contributes to depression. They're under constant stress, they don't eat healthy foods, they don't sleep enough, and they don't exercise. College students have exceedingly high expectations for themselves, and few can meet their lofty ambitions.

The occasional bad day is normal. As much as you hate for

your child to be unhappy, students sometimes need to wallow in self-pity and misery for a few days. Before you overreact about your child's mood, look for evidence that he is making friends, attending classes on a regular basis, and participating in campus activities. As long as your child is maintaining a normal schedule and can talk about activities, friends, and what's going on in classes, things are probably all right. But keep checking.

Clinical depression, along with depression prompted by stressful situations, can bring on suicidal thoughts. Warning signs of depression include evidence that your child is pulling away from friends and family, using drugs or alcohol to excess, refusing to participate in favorite activities, or is feeling especially disappointed or dissatisfied with himself. Stress-induced depression can result from a financial crisis, academic failure, the breakup of a relationship, trouble with the law, the death of a friend or family member, or issues about sexual orientation.

Suicide is the second leading cause of death among college students, behind only accidental death. If you have any indication your child is thinking about suicide, let her know that you're concerned, and urge her to talk to a counselor or physician. If there is evidence that she has made a suicide attempt or is planning to, insist that she see a health professional. If necessary, take her yourself, or ask a college staff member or campus security to conduct a wellness check.

For more information about parents' role in college mental health, check the Jed Foundation website: https://www.jedfoundation.org/.

Anxiety: Everyone feels anxious sometimes. It's normal to be nervous about giving a presentation in class or feeling uncomfortable about whether you just said something you shouldn't have. Sometimes anxiety is even helpful. It can be a warning sign if you're in danger and can spur you to react.

Anxiety disorder is something else altogether, and it is the most common mental illness in the United States.[21] It's a constant, extreme feeling of unease and dread that can interfere with daily life. Rather than inspiring students to prepare for a test or figure out how to prevent an argument with a friend, it can prevent them from identifying any course of action at all. Some students stop attending class, hanging out with friends, or getting on a bus due to fears that they can't even put into words.

Anxiety disorder can manifest in physical illness as well. Headaches, stomach pains, nausea, rapid heartbeat, and shortness of breath are sometimes caused by anxiety and provide even more reasons to be anxious. The good news is that anxiety is considered the most treatable of mental health conditions, and the college mental health service can help.

WHEN THE PROBLEMS ARE TOO SERIOUS TO IGNORE

If an injury or illness keeps a student out of the classroom for more than two weeks, the best step may be to consider dropping at least one course so that he can focus on the rest of his classes. In these situations, academic advisers encourage students to think about the kinds of classes they're taking and how hard it is to make up the assignments they're missing. Lecture classes and courses that rely primarily on reading and writing tend to be more flexible. Language, math, or lab courses, on the other hand, rely heavily on in-class learning. It's hard for a student to keep up with the material if several sessions are missed, and it's unfair to the other students in the class to slow the pace for one person.

Students worry that dropping a class means they will fall too

---

21. Anxiety and Depression Association of America, "Facts and Statistics," https://adaa.org/about-adaa/press-room/facts-statistics (accessed July 23, 2019).

far behind on the college time line. "If I don't have fifteen credits this semester, there's no way I can graduate in four years." "I can't drop that class—it's the first course in a two-year sequence, and I can only take it fall semester. I'll be a whole year behind."

Certainly, there are downsides to dropping a class, but overworking during a serious illness may result in poor performance in *every* class. A dropped class might require a few months of summer school or even an extra year of college. The question is whether taking time to recover will mean academic success rather than failure, or health rather than lingering illness. This is a case where taking additional time to finish school might be the wise choice.

ROAD HAZARDS: THE COMMUTING LIFE

In some ways, commuter students face fewer health-related adjustments than dorm dwellers. If they're living with their family, they sleep in their own beds, eat home-cooked meals, and avoid the shared germs in residence halls. When they're sick, they even have the option of seeing their family physician, and they have help from mom and dad.

That does not mean that commuters are risk-free. Riding on buses and subways puts them in close contact with their fellow passengers' illnesses, and students who drive long distances to school tend to eat more than their share of greasy, fat-laden fast foods. The backseat of a commuter's car, strewn with beverage cans and sandwich wrappers, provides evidence of diet deficiencies. Moreover, students who live off campus are less likely to receive age-based health information—those wellness programs that are routinely presented in residence halls, sororities, and fraternities.

The commute itself contributes to the stress of school. Commuters' schedules are segmented, and balancing work, home, and school can be challenging. Commuters struggle to find enough time in the day to do justice to all the demands. What's more, the frustrations add up as they try to work on assignments at home, only to find the notes they need are in a locker on campus. Or they plan to do their homework over the lunch hour at work, but then remember they left their packet of reading materials at home.

Even with parents close by to oversee their health, commuter students push themselves beyond endurance, then multitask in the car on the way to school, eating, drinking, and practicing a presentation while hurrying to make it to class on time.

Commuters are convinced that no one recognizes all the stress and extra responsibility they face. "Everyone thinks my life is so easy, but it's not! No one understands how hard it is to juggle school, a job, and everything at home."

Parents of commuters have a better chance than most to see when the stress is greatest and to find ways to ease the pressure. Veronica's mother offered to drive her daughter to campus during midterms and finals, giving her child a chance to study on the way to school and relax on the way home. When she picked Veronica up on the last day of finals, they went to dinner to celebrate.

Neil's parents declared that Sundays meant no family obligations or chores—he could do homework or use that as a day off if he wanted to.

The greatest stress reliever for commuter students is for their family to recognize that they're working hard and to give them an occasional break.

EMERGENCY ALARM: CRISIS ON CAMPUS

Campus emergencies do happen. Knowing that, families want assurance that their students will be safe.

Few businesses or industries have security plans as multifaceted and transparent as colleges and universities. Most campuses have their own police or security force, trained responders, counselors, health care providers, formal policies and procedures, and staffing assignments for handling all kinds of emergency situations. Annual conferences of higher education professionals consistently include programs on how to handle a campus crisis, including crisis communication planning and active-shooter response training. Emergency protocols are outlined for evacuations, lockdowns, or quarantines. In an emergency a college campus may be one of the safest places to be.

At most schools, students are automatically signed up to receive safety messages by text, phone, email, or all three. Parents should be able to sign up for those messages as well, either on the same platform or on a separate system. With every student carrying a cell phone, though, it's possible that families will hear about an emergency from their student or even through a news report before getting a message from the school.

In a time of crisis, the first response must be to secure and protect the immediate area and ensure medical attention for any victims. The next responsibility is reaching out to students and others in the vicinity to provide instructions on what they should do. Determining the cause of the crisis and crafting a message for the public requires coordination with police and first responders, and that may take time. Handling phone calls from parents and providing reassurance about their students are important commitments, but securing the area, controlling the situation, and establishing accurate information come first.

QUICK TIPS FOR STUDENTS

- Prevention is the best medicine. You already know the basic health messages: eat some fruits and vegetables

every day, drink plenty of water, sleep at least seven
hours a night (eight is better), and exercise.

- Especially during cold and flu season, wash your hands
  frequently. Keep a cautious distance from friends and
  roommates when they're sick—but be kind. Bring
  them soup from the dining center and offer to pick
  up some juice and tissues from the convenience store.
- When you start to feel sick, give yourself a break.
  Don't try to fight through the aches and pains. Take a
  nap; drink even more water and some juice. Call the
  health clinic or the school's "nurse line" and ask for
  advice—should you make an appointment to see a
  doctor? Should you be taking any medication? Then
  follow their advice.
- Watch for signs of stress. If you notice that you frequently feel anxious or depressed, have trouble sleeping, lose your appetite or can't stop eating, or if you
  have persistent headaches or stomachaches, make an
  appointment to talk to a doctor.
- Colleges usually provide access to counselors and
  therapists. Use the resources.
- Alcohol, tobacco, and long weekends of partying take
  their toll on health. Look for less hazardous ways to
  have fun.

CHAPTER 10

Singing in Choir, Studying in Senegal

Learning Outside the Classroom

When high school students are applying to college, they know that listing accomplishments in sports, the arts, or community involvement will improve their application. They also know it helps to be well-rounded and dependable, so they continue with activities like Boy Scouts or the library's teen book club when they would just as soon quit. And they're told to show how they're contributing to their college expenses, which means an after-school job or giving up Saturdays to coach soccer. Their weeks are full, and their heads are spinning.

By the time they arrive at college, some students are so burned out that they spend their entire first month on campus trying to beat the high score in a video game. They tell themselves they don't need to be involved in any campus activities yet because they have to concentrate on their studies. The truth is, they're relieved to finally have a moment to themselves.

One day, though, they emerge from their room, looking for something to do. The options are staggering. The student activities office boasts about its four hundred student organizations.

How to decide? "Student council in high school was kind of fun. What do you have to do to get into student government here?" they wonder. "My philosophy professor said he's the adviser for the chess club. Maybe I should ask him about that." "It's amazing to watch the rowing team on the river in the morning. I'd like to try out, but how do I learn to row?"

SO MANY CHOICES, SO LITTLE TIME

What students learn in clubs and organizations can help them clarify their career interests. Justin was questioning his major in engineering, believing it would mean a lifetime of solitude sitting in front of a computer. When he joined the school's solar car team, he discovered that collaboration and idea sharing are critical components in the engineering design process.

Student activities also offer a chance to explore different approaches to a major. At the information fair during orientation, Beatrice tried to point her daughter toward the college newspaper's information booth, but Lucie, a journalism major, paused to look at the brochures promoting the school's Ecology Club. "I don't think I want to work on the paper this year," Lucie said. "It was fun in high school, but I heard it takes way more time in college. I like writing, but I really don't like the business side of running a newspaper. Remember when I wrote that story last year on recycling, and I interviewed the owner of the recycling company? This poster says they're looking for bloggers and marketers to help promote sustainability. I'm just going to ask a couple of questions about how I might fit in. I'll catch up with you in a few minutes."

Parents look through the lists of student organizations and see a number of groups that seem intriguing, some that raise red flags, and some that raise only questions. "Disc golf sounds like fun." "Canoe Battleship Club? That can't end well." "How does anyone decide between the aikido club, karate club, and tae kwon do?"

Parents can rarely predict which organization might make the most difference in their child's life—perhaps a group that addresses politics, health and wellness, gender identity, religion, or a purely social group called Pancake Club that meets at a nearby diner on Saturday mornings.

The most successful and satisfied students invest time and energy on campus. Generally, students join organizations because of a particular interest, they want to meet like-minded students, or they're looking for personal or career development opportunities. In simple terms, they want to meet people and have fun, and they'd like to try something new. The college becomes a home when they make a commitment to some segment of the school through their involvement. They find their own smaller community within the larger campus.

A COMMUTER'S HOME ON CAMPUS

All the benefits of campus involvement apply doubly to commuter students. Joining a club or organization helps commuters meet and make friends. The student council office or the gym provides a place to hang out between classes. Membership in a group convinces commuters that college isn't just a place to park the car and attend class; it's where they belong.

Jillian's mother noticed that her daughter's entire outlook toward college changed when she joined the gospel choir. "I think that living at home made it hard for her to meet people until she made that connection to a group. Rehearsals don't start until seven at night, so she had to stay on campus after her last class. Within a couple of weeks, she was going out for dinner with a few of the other singers before practice. They've turned out to be some of her best friends. Music isn't her major. She's actually in food science, but she says the gospel group is the best part of college."

JUST DO IT

The place to start getting involved on campus is wherever the student feels at least a little bit comfortable. Someone who enjoyed band or baseball in high school may not be headed toward a major in music or a position on the college team, but he may still want to practice his saxophone or play ball. He can sign up for the pep band that performs for the women's basketball team or join an intramural sports club.

College activities offer a chance to try something a student might never previously have considered. A midwesterner who enrolls at the University of California, Los Angeles, can join a surfing club, and the Mississippi native at Northern Vermont University can join a ski and snowboard club. The sense of adventure and accomplishment that comes with learning a new skill or stepping into the unknown makes participation an adventure.

Students can also find opportunities that don't require a long-term commitment, or in some cases, not even much personal effort. They shouldn't feel that every activity must have a life-altering outcome; a Friday evening workshop at the student union might offer lessons in paper making or pot throwing, but it may never lead to a decision to join the art club that sponsored the program.

Often a student's personal skills and talents provide an unexpected opening into involvement opportunities. Experience in Web design might be exactly what the law club is looking for in their efforts to update their online image. Artistic ability may be the inroad to the political science club, which needs Get Out the Vote posters for the coming election.

Ideally, the first year of college is a chance to sample the opportunities and begin to make choices. Students should try a few different groups with the idea that they're under no obligation to commit long-term. The second year is a time to sort through the freshman experiences and determine which groups hold the most appeal. As interests and abilities change, students may find a new group that's the best fit yet. Sophomores and juniors begin serving in leadership positions or at least doing more of the active work of the group—helping schedule games and select equipment for a sports club or organizing readings for the campus literary society. As upperclassmen, students can shape improvements for the future of the organization and encourage newer members as emerging leaders.

SEE THE WORLD! BUT LEAVE MY FRIENDS?

The promise of studying abroad is a strong selling point for students selecting a college. A school that offers a semester of study in a hilltop castle in France rises to the top of the wish list. Often, though, while the dream of going abroad is always floating gently on the horizon, it's hard to take the leap and schedule a semester away from campus.

Students see the value of study abroad, but the downside is leaving friends, interrupting a budding relationship, or figuring out how to sublet an apartment for part of the year. Those students who decide to take the risk, however, almost always come home with visions of going abroad again. "It was the best thing I've ever done," they rave. "It changed my life."

Short-term study abroad programs allow wary students to sample international opportunities without making the commitment of a whole semester or longer. These two- or three-week trips are popular over January terms or for part of the summer, and students can earn a few credits while studying with a professor from their own school.

Short-term programs have their benefits: they cost less than a full semester; they take up the same number of words on a résumé; and the students might all be from the home school and already in classes together. However, short programs lack the deep experience of full-semester programs. The longer programs allow students to immerse themselves, rather than just visit, another country and culture. The odds are better for meeting students from other schools and from the destination country, offering a richer experience. Students learn the exhilaration of solving complex problems on their own. And they may discover the deep pleasure of solitude and find that they are their own best companion.

Key to committing to either a short- or long-term study abroad program is considering how it will affect the overall cost of college and the student's progress toward a degree. Both short- and long-term programs are available that support specific academic majors, allowing students to earn required architecture credits while touring Italy or completing engineering credits at a university in Australia. Other programs offer electives, taught in English, that fulfill general education requirements that will count toward graduation.

Any learning abroad experience requires careful thought before selecting a destination and a program. Among the questions that students and parents should consider:

- What part of the world does your student want to visit? What does she know about the politics, culture, and climate of the region?
- What kind of predeparture information will the student receive? Does someone talk to participants about cultural issues and safety? What information is addressed when students first arrive in the country?
- Is there a predeparture or introductory program for parents?

- What kind of student services and support does the program provide? Who will help if something goes wrong?
- How do students communicate with family and friends while they're abroad?
- Does your student have the language skills to be comfortable in another country? When students are not proficient in the language, the first weeks of classes will be difficult and exhausting.
- How does the cost of study abroad compare with staying on the home campus? What extra expenses should families expect, beyond tuition and program fees, airfare, and room and board? Do student scholarships apply to the study abroad program?
- How long does your student want to stay abroad? Will she arrive early to travel or explore? Will she stay after the program ends? Does she plan to travel on weekends or holidays while she's there? Changes in these plans after the student arrives can mean the anticipated budget will not cover the expenses.
- Is the program affiliated with the student's college or university? If not, credits may not transfer.
- What classes will students be taking? How many credits will apply toward graduation? What are the steps to have international credits applied back home?
- Where will students live? On a campus, in a family home, in an apartment? Is housing in a big city, small village, or rural area?

A student's housing options require more than passing consideration. The study abroad office at your student's college will have information about the choices at each destination, but students should not assume that the terms "dormitory," "apartment," or "homestay" are self-explanatory. A dormitory in another country might be very different from what the student expects. It may house students from multiple universities and be a thirty-minute bus ride from classes. An apartment or flat could house only American students, and your son or daughter might never socialize with local students or speak anything but English outside of classes. A homestay gives students a chance to improve their language skills, but the families who host them sometimes are not the families they imagined. Students may find themselves living with a newly married couple just a few years older than they are; an elderly couple who are renting out their spare bedroom for the stipend they receive; or a bustling family with five children, two dogs, and a chaotic lifestyle that leaves little time to interact with an American college student.

A homestay can be the best learning opportunity, but students may need to be flexible about their needs and expectations. Marta, an international programs adviser, recalled a conversation she had with a young man who was preparing for a semester in Argentina. "My mom is worried I might end up with a family who's not used to feeding a six-foot, two-hundred-pound American boy. She's afraid I won't get enough to eat," he said. "I do eat a lot, I guess, but I can just plan to buy food and keep it in my bedroom."

Marta was able to sort through the list of homestay families and worked with the program coordinator in Argentina on the match. They found a husband and wife who not only understood the calorie intake of a still-growing young adult, but whose home was above their family restaurant, where he could order lunches and dinners off a menu.

Another student, Marta said, was hoping for a family with children who would help her learn more of the language. She was matched with a family with two teenagers who were much too busy with their friends to spend time with the student. Fortunately, the family's eight-year-old loved reading children's books and playing games with her.

The cost for a semester's study abroad could be a little less than the cost of a semester at the home college, or it could be double that amount. Although you don't want to go further in debt for your child's study abroad experience, students shouldn't try to live on a bare-bones budget. The student who lives in London for three months and can't afford an occasional half-price theater ticket or a day trip to Stonehenge will be frustrated by missing some of the obvious benefits of the experience. One of the common problems for students, though, is piling up debt while they're abroad. They learn that their college in Belgium is just a fast-train ride to Berlin or the Riviera, and every weekend they're on a train for a new destination. Since "this is the chance of a lifetime," they buy shoes in Italy or a watch in Zurich.

Study abroad has particular benefits for commuter students. Bethany lived at home during her freshman and sophomore years, but the first semester of her junior year, she signed up for a program in Costa Rica. Besides giving her a chance to work on her Spanish requirement, this was the first time she had lived with students her own age. "It was an adjustment at first to live with a houseful of other students," she said, "but it was so much fun. Sometimes we would just sit and talk for hours on end. The whole experience of studying abroad was great, but I especially liked living with other students."

STUDY ABROAD IN DEVELOPING COUNTRIES

Even those parents who have delivered their child to a college a thousand miles away will hesitate when they put their student on a plane to a country they know little about. Clara's mother always imagined her daughter would go to Paris—after all, she was getting a minor in French. She was taken by complete surprise when Clara told her she was looking at a program in Senegal.

"Senegal?" her mother asked. "I don't think I could even find that on a map. Why do you want to go there?"

"My roommate's sister went last year, and it's a great program, Mom. The classes are taught in French, so I can practice my language. Plus the last six weeks is an internship. I'm thinking I want to get a master's degree in public health after I graduate," Clara explained, "and this program offers an internship with a community health program. It will really help when I apply to grad school."

A Web search provided Clara's mother with reassurance that the program in Senegal was accredited and had an excellent reputation. Her daughter would have the advice and assistance of study abroad staff in case of any problems, and the internship seemed like a valuable add-on.

Still, it's scary to send a child that far away. Any news of international acts of terrorism naturally raise parents' concerns. A mother called the day after seeing reports of violence in the country where her son was planning to study. "I saw the news reports about flare-ups in Kenya. My son is supposed to go there next month. Should you be sending students there?"

Colleges and universities promote international study as one of the most important ways to increase global understanding. American students who spend time in other countries come home with a better grasp of the connections between cultures and economies around the world. But is it safe?

Advisers of reputable programs do not recommend study abroad in any area deemed dangerous, and they will provide thorough background information on the culture and politics of the area students will be visiting. In Kenya, the flare-up was an isolated incident, far from the city where students were staying. Staff members would be on-site to talk with students about local and international issues and to provide assistance in case of any emergency. They would instruct students on how to maintain a respectful presence and a low profile, and they would talk about safety precautions, including avoiding any dangerous areas.

Parents can worry themselves sick over all the possible (but unlikely) problems, but careful planning will take care of most troubles:

- Confirm current travel safety information at travel .state.gov and search for travelers health information at the Centers for Disease Control, www.cdc.gov.
- The study abroad program will advise students on immunizations and other medical precautions needed for the area where they will be studying. Students must have health insurance coverage overseas. If the study abroad office provides an insurance policy, compare it with your own to make sure your student has the best coverage. If possible, arrange for a policy that includes family emergency transportation, allowing a family member to travel to the destination in case of a serious illness or accident, along with emergency medical evacuation to bring the student home if necessary. Travel abroad programs are likely to provide this type of coverage.
- Students can assign power of attorney to you or another responsible adult for the duration of the program. Power of attorney allows you to take care of transactions your student may not be able to handle from a distance, such as financial aid, banking, insurance, fund transfers, and income tax filing.
- Be sure *you* have a valid and updated passport. In case of an emergency, you will not want to take time to renew or apply for a passport.

- Make arrangements ahead of time for how you will communicate with your student. Not all issues can be handled over Web video formats. If significant problems like lost luggage and missed flights result in lengthy phone calls, you will avoid astronomical bills by adding international rates to your cell phone plan.

OVERSEAS PITFALLS

Although parents worry most about accidents and illnesses while their student is abroad, the greatest dangers students face come from their own choices. An eighteen-year-old can drink alcohol legally in many countries, and marijuana is legal—or not penalized—in a number of countries. This often leads to excess, but other cultures have little tolerance for drunk or stoned Americans. Students can find themselves in deep trouble with their hosts or confronted by police for intoxication or drug use.

Students who are arrested while abroad can end up in jail, facing court procedures in a legal system and language they don't fully understand. Before the trip, students will hear from their study abroad advisers about the laws in the country where they will be, but students don't always heed the warnings.

Academic failure is another factor. Students believe their work will be judged less critically when they are studying abroad. "The professors know we're not going to study," they think. "They have to know we're here for the total experience."

International universities have somewhat different teaching styles, and a student may find that courses are more difficult than at home. In addition, the temptation is strong to skip classes. "When will I ever have the chance again to go to Oktoberfest in Munich?" Classes can drop in priority with all the tempting alternatives. If students benefit from grade inflation in U.S. colleges, the strict grade policies in another country will be a surprise. Students need to remember that a prerequisite for a future class, admission into a graduate program, scholarship qualifications, and future jobs can all be affected by poor performance in an international program.

DEALING WITH THE UPS AND DOWNS

After Naomi learned she'd been accepted for a summer study abroad program in Morocco, she called home to tell her parents the exciting news. "This is going to be amazing! I can't wait. I wish I could leave tomorrow!"

A week later, she was on the verge of dropping out of the program. "I can't go to Morocco. It's about 110 degrees there in the summer. I don't know about the food—I don't think I like it—and I'm not sure they treat American women very well."

The mood swings students undergo before they travel abroad are only a precursor to the emotional fluctuations they will suffer during the first few days after they arrive. Studying abroad can be exhausting and unsettling. By the time your daughter finds a place where she can finally send you a message, she's likely to be tired, homesick, and discouraged. Just like those first calls home during the freshman year, you will only hear about the negative experiences. You'll want to transfer funds for a return ticket right away. But before you do, stop and think about it.

Remind yourself—and your student—that she has already made some significant strides. She did, after all, figure out how to contact you. She probably has located a cash machine. The small accomplishments that meant little or nothing back home feel like major achievements in a new land and a new language.

When they're in an unfamiliar setting, students establish routines quickly to help them feel more comfortable. They're compulsive about checking for their keys before they leave their room in the morning. A daily trip to the bakery for bread and to the greengrocer for fresh vegetables becomes a ritual. They'll make an effort to board the same bus each day in order to see a familiar face in the driver's seat.

As life falls into a pattern, students begin to feel more secure. With every new success, they gain confidence. They learn that local residents can understand them, even if their grammar and diction are not perfect. They can forget about their first attempt to order a cup of coffee and laugh at themselves when they realize they've just asked the price of a library, not the cost of a book. They dare to make mistakes, and they find ways to correct their errors.

Students returning from study abroad typically face culture shock while they readjust to life back at home. They may resent the trendy stores where they once bought all their clothes; now they cling to the poncho or the knit cap they bartered for at the Saturday market. They talk for hours on end about the people they met and the places they visited—or they sit sullenly in front of the computer, writing poetry or blogging about their time abroad.

Students are changed by international travel in ways they can't entirely explain, and they believe that friends and family cannot possibly understand. They might be more critical, more serious, and more reclusive for a time, but will gradually put it all into a healthy perspective.

STUDY ABROAD: AN EDUCATION FOR THE FAMILY

The more you learn about your child's travel abroad destination, the more you'll want to explore it for yourself. Watching your student function in a different culture can be one of the most gratifying experiences of parenting a young adult. Seeing that your son has mastered the train system in Spain or your daughter can read a ferry schedule in Greek is heartwarming proof of your child's adaptability and independence.

If you decide to visit your student during an international experience, however, don't interrupt the program's academic schedule. Most study abroad programs require students to be in classes or meetings a large part of their day. And students need time with their classmates. They're all working through the same issues, and the support they offer one another is invaluable.

Still, a well-timed visit from parents can be welcome, especially when students are longing for the sound of a familiar accent or wishing they didn't have to miss a holiday at home. By following a few guidelines, you can make a family visit rewarding for you and your child.

- If you can schedule your arrival for a weekend, your student won't immediately have to choose between you and classes. Be prepared for role reversal while your son or daughter takes the lead, showing you where things are and how things work.
- Keep in mind that you may be on vacation, but your student is not. Don't spend more than a few days with your student, and don't take up all his time any day you're there. Take this opportunity to do some exploring on your own.
- If you plan to tour as a family following the semester, let your student finish the program before you arrive. And be prepared for some letdown after students have said good-bye to their classmates and hosts.

Domestic Alternatives to Study Abroad

For the student who isn't comfortable with the concept of international study, or if finances are a concern, many of the same benefits are available without crossing an ocean or even using a passport. National student exchange programs let students attend another college within the United States for a semester or a year. The Oklahoma State student who hopes to someday work in New England can take a semester of environmental science courses at Colby College in Maine and get the best of both schools. A student from North Carolina State can do an internship in media studies in Minneapolis.

Students also can explore the unknown in their own backyard. A student attending school in a large city can tutor recent immigrants who are learning English, while discovering a different culture just across town.

For information, see https://www.nse.org/.

LEARNING BY DOING: COMMUNITY SERVICE

One day your son mentions that he's earning extra credit for his business ethics class by packing box lunches for an AIDS organization, and you can't help but wonder: Whatever happened to lectures and exams? Your daughter calls home to say she's going to raise funds for the homeless by living for a week in a refrigerator carton on the college lawn. She's probably thinking this will be a great time with friends for a noble cause. You're probably worrying about her safety, her studies, and her sanity.

Colleges and universities often incorporate service learning and community projects into the curriculum. A pre-law class might include helping Somali immigrants study for a citizenship test. A women's studies class might ask students to interview women who are involved in local politics.

A well-planned service learning project not only provides opportunities for students to observe and participate in real-life situations, but it also includes discussion and reflection on the experience. As young adults test their idealism against some of life's reality, an instructor or adviser will be talking about their impressions and emotions. Frequently students are asked to write a journal or blog of their activities and reactions, and those impressions are shared with the instructor and classmates. The comments from other students can be particularly reassuring and supportive as individuals recognize that their responses are not so unusual.

If your student tells you he will be doing a service learning project, he should be able to discuss the following:

- How do students get to the site? How will they get home?
- Is there supervision at the site? What kind of support and guidance do students have from a faculty member or adviser? Who do students talk to if they have questions?
- What are the goals of the project? What is the student's role in the project?
- What does the student develop, produce, or turn in at the end of the project (for example, a report, journal, or proposal for change)?

QUICK TIPS FOR STUDENTS
- As they told you at orientation, join something! Try one safe bet—something you liked in high school. If you enjoy sports, check out what's available at the

campus recreation center. If you were in the orchestra, find out if there's an ensemble group you can join. Also try one completely new activity. Can't find what you want? Ask your academic adviser for a suggestion, or ask your residence adviser if there's something you can volunteer to do in the dorm.

- If the group you join doesn't turn out to be a good fit, quit and try something else. If someone tries to pressure you to stay, make your decision based on what's right for you.

- Don't overcommit. It's important to be involved, but it's easy to be pulled into too many activities. Classes come first, then save time for studying and for being with friends. Clubs and sports should be fun, not add to the stress in your life.

- Think about studying abroad, doing a national exchange program, or participating in a service learning project. Most students discover they learn more from these programs than any of their classes—partly because they're *using* what they learned in the classroom.

CHAPTER 11

"What Have You Done?"

When Social Choices Clash with Family Values

Throughout adolescence, teens are bumping up against the boundaries their parents have set for them and defying house rules. At the college level, they continue this journey toward autonomy, sometimes defying family values and making choices their parents don't expect.

In early November, Sharon drove to campus to bring her daughter home for a farewell dinner before her grandparents moved south for the winter. When Carla came to the dorm lobby to meet her, Sharon barely recognized her. She hadn't seen Carla in two months, and she had no warning that her daughter's light brown hair was now dyed ink black with purple highlights. More surprising, it was shaved on one side, revealing a palette of silver hoops and geometric studs lining her right ear. Carla was wearing a long black skirt, shredded at the hem. The cute, brightly colored parka that Carla started school with in the fall had been replaced by a shapeless, floor-length wool coat, and Sharon could track her daughter's footsteps by the clopping of her thick-soled boots as she dashed off to say good-bye to friends.

The ride home wasn't at all what Sharon had been looking forward to. She had anticipated a pleasant conversation about Carla's classes, campus life, and preparations for the next day's family gathering. As soon as they got into the car, though, Carla announced that she needed a nap. "I had a paper due today, so I didn't get much sleep the past couple of nights." Then she slumped down in the seat and closed her eyes.

When they arrived at home, Sharon fixed a quick supper. As she offered Carla a taste of the pasta sauce, she flinched when she spotted two round, gold studs piercing her daughter's tongue. All her questions came out in one loud burst of disapproval. "What is *this*? Have you punctured every part of your body? These clothes—where did they come from? And your hair! This is just not *you*!"

Although Carla's new look was a huge surprise to her mother, it didn't seem particularly dramatic to Carla. After the initial blowup, Carla reminded her mother that she began college with two piercings in each ear, and Sharon had gone with her when she got them. Adding a few more to one ear didn't seem like such a big issue.

Soon after she moved to campus, Carla explained, she and her friends had discovered a nearby thrift shop, and she gradually built up a new collection of clothes. "They hardly cost anything at all. You can get real bargains at thrift shops, you know."

The coat, she said, was perfect for winter. "The pockets are huge. I can fit my phone, tablet, and water bottle in the pockets. I don't even need a backpack."

Her haircut was a Halloween makeover, and she decided she liked it enough to keep it for a while. "It's hair. It grows out," she reminded her mother.

She admitted the tongue piercing might seem a bit much, but compared to the people she lived with, it wasn't all that unusual. On her floor in the residence hall, Carla said, there were at least four kids with eyebrow piercings, a couple had pierced lips, and "almost everyone is getting a nose piercing."

"Mom, some kids have body jewelry in places you wouldn't even think could be pierced. And don't worry about my tongue. After I freak out my high school friends over winter break, I'm taking the studs out and letting the holes grow in. It's kind of weird, feeling them in my mouth all the time."

WHAT REBELLION LOOKS LIKE

During their own college years, today's parents might have rebelled against their families' standards by getting tattoos of a Chinese symbol, a butterfly, or a twining wrist bracelet. No one is surprised anymore to see mothers at family weekend with an ankle tattoo or a small diamond nose stud. There's rarely a second glance at fathers with pierced ears or full arm tattoos. Over the years, they may have added an image symbolizing the birth of their children or some other life event. Plenty of parents helped their daughters design their first tattoo or took their sons for ear piercings. Nevertheless, seeing their college student's new branding or body jewelry may be a surprise and a disappointment—not because they had it done but because they didn't call home first to talk it over.

Some families might consider any body art or dramatic change in appearance to be a significant act of rebellion, but a poll of parents indicates that for many, it's more a matter of nuance. They would be more upset if their child went to a less-than-sterile tattoo shop, selected a piercing or tattoo that might be visible during a job interview, or got "too much body art." For others, piercings or tattoos are not the concern; they worry more about behavioral acts of rebellion—refusing to communicate with the family, smoking, drinking, doing drugs, or rejecting family values.

Compared to years past, the current generation of students

is less likely than their parents were to actively rebel against the family or society in general. Still, a lot of students like to try out new appearances, use their body for artistic expression, or experiment with an unusual hair color or makeup scheme. While a major change to appearance or attitude could indicate shifting values, consider the big picture. Is your student communicating with you? Doing well enough in school? Involved in activities and excited about college? And keep in mind that you may not be so innocent yourself. As one mother noted, "I had a reunion with some of my college friends last year, and we all went home afterward with matching fish tattoos. Apparently, peer pressure can affect you at any age."

ADJUSTING WHEN YOUR CHILD COMES HOME

The first year of college is as much about new experiences as it is about academics. In high school, students may have avoided anyone who seemed "different." Now, living alongside dozens of new people, they find the differences interesting. They learn that the star athlete, who a year ago would have been labeled arrogant, is committed to social justice, and the eccentric kid wearing a safari helmet has a wonderful, wry sense of humor.

In some ways it's like being back in eighth grade—a chance to meet new people and try on different personas to see what fits and who responds. Students can adjust their image entirely from one day to the next, dressing in artsy black for a poetry slam on Tuesday evening, putting on a business suit for an internship in town on weekday mornings, and wearing school colors for the game on Saturday. And in each transformation, they can still be themselves and still be surrounded by supportive friends.

As it turns out, it's returning home that can make students

question who they are and where they belong. Major flare-ups can erupt the first time they come home after starting college. You and your student might have very different ideas on who is in charge of the schedule during your student's weekend or vacation visit. You might have made plans to stop at a nice restaurant for dinner to break up the ride home, but when you arrive at the residence hall, you see that your son and his roommate are finishing off the last of a three-foot submarine sandwich. You've invited the relatives for a family dinner, but your daughter made arrangements to meet up with a friend from high school. "I have other plans. I'm meeting up with Angela. She's picking me up in twenty minutes."

You've been waiting for your child to come home, but after a few days, you find yourself incredibly annoyed at her behavior. "She hasn't picked up a single dish, she left a pile of dirty clothes in the laundry room, and she's completely self-absorbed. How did we raise such a spoiled princess?"

Meanwhile, your student is baffled by the emotions she's feeling about being home. The family is not like she remembered. She notices that you seem to be closer to her younger sister than you used to be, and you're talking about neighbors she's never even heard of. Things feel different, because things *are* different.

College students refuse to revert to the teen rules of reporting where they're going and when they'll be home. Parents want their children to fit back into the old, comfortable family routines, while students want to hear that their visit home is special. "You said you missed me. I thought you'd be happy to have me around. I didn't know I was just coming home to vacuum the living room and walk the dog." And parents don't understand why the only things their sons or daughters seem to appreciate about being home are the bathroom, the refrigerator, and your car.

Minimizing the Mishaps of the Student Visit

- If you will be picking up your student from school, clarify what time you expect to arrive, what time you want to start home, and any plans you've made for the drive or for when you get home.
- Talk to your student about how much he will be bringing home. You might think this is just a brief visit, and he can fit everything into a duffel bag. He might have saved up a month's worth of laundry, and he's decided this is a good time to bring home his skateboard and the three-dimensional design project that earned him an A in robotics. Allow some time to pack the car, as well as extra time for friends to say good-bye.
- Discuss in advance any family obligations, use of the car, curfews, and information sharing you're expecting while your student is at home. Ask about your student's plans, explaining that you want to make arrangements that work for everyone in the household.
- Be prepared for a quiet ride home. The days leading up to school breaks are hectic. You'll seem like the best parent ever if you bring along a blanket and pillow for the car.
- Students may sleep more during breaks than seems normal. They're exhausted by dorm life and exams; it feels comforting to be back in their own bed; and most important, retreating to the bedroom is a way to gradually work back into the rhythms and pace of being home.
- Recognize that some of your student's disagreeable behaviors are not a rejection of you and your values, but they serve as a way to communicate independence.

THE COMMUTER'S ADJUSTMENTS

If students live at home and commute to school, their increasing independence is no less challenging. It may be even more difficult because the whole family will be living with the conflicts on a daily basis.

Like Carla, Janette's son changed his clothing style during his first few months of school. Instead of his former standard outfit of jeans and a T-shirt or sweatshirt, he was now wearing dark, turtleneck shirts and black pants. One weekend he hauled boxes of his old clothes down to the basement.

"I don't have room for these," he said. "I'm moving my desk into my closet. I found a small couch at a yard sale, and I'm putting it in my room. I need my own study space."

It wasn't so much the clothes and the redecorating that bothered Janette. Her son had been a fairly traditional high school student, participating in track and cross-country, the debate team, and band. Now it seemed like all he cared about was music and movies. And his schedule changed; on weekends, he was going out at about the time Janette went to bed and coming home in the early hours of the morning.

One night Janette wasn't sure whether he had come home at all. When he showed up for dinner the following evening, she confronted him. "You can't stay out until all hours like this. If you're not coming home, you really have to tell me. I know you're not in high school anymore, but I still need to know you're okay."

"Mom, most of my friends don't see their parents from one holiday to the next," he replied. "You know you can trust me. I'm not going to check in with you all the time."

It's not living away from home that changes college students. College coincides with a time in the lives of young adults when they are taking bigger and bolder steps on their own. Separation from the family is a natural and necessary step for young adults. The challenge for everyone involved is how to adjust to that separation while still finding a path to stay connected.

It's true that you have the right to establish ground rules, but you also need to recognize your child's increasing maturity and all the obligations in his life. A commuter's social commitments are interwoven with work and school. Study groups, going out with friends, and dating are all part of the package.

When students live at home, parents expect to rely on them for some basic responsibilities. Sunday dinner might seem like a tradition to you, not an imposition. From your student's standpoint, it feels like one more obligation in an already overscheduled week. While you sometimes have to accept the absences, you can also make a claim for family participation and basic respect.

CULTURE CLASH

Education is much more than the process of gathering facts and theories. It's also about examining and integrating lessons into life. College-age students are opening their eyes and their minds to the ideas and lifestyles of the friends they're meeting, the professors they're listening to, and the authors they're reading. Inevitably, they will begin to see their own experiences and their family's values in new ways.

The beliefs and routines that they have always taken as truth are now questioned and tested. Whether students focus on the religion they were brought up in, the family's politics, or their parents' economic decisions, family members can hardly help but take personal offense. It's upsetting to have your child challenge your beliefs, and it's disappointing to see behaviors you disapprove of.

Minnesota psychologist Scott Slattery suggests that parents respond to their suddenly unfamiliar student as they would a foreign exchange student. "If you had a visitor staying with you from some other country, and he wore clothes that were different from what you're used to or had a hairstyle that was different from what you typically see, you probably wouldn't be offended," Slattery says. "You might be curious about it, and maybe you'd find a way to politely ask about it."

Slattery suggests that parents try the same approach with their student. "Talk about what you're noticing and ask if a lot of students at college wear their hair like this, or if the symbol on your son's necklace has a particular meaning."

College students are not slow-witted. They'll pick up on the sarcasm, but they'll also appreciate that you're asking about their college experience and reminding them of family routines, rather than accusing them of doing something wrong or stoically pretending that nothing has changed.

Students make significant developmental growth over the course of their college years. They're going through a process of examining their past, present, and future. They're figuring out who they are, testing new ideas, and discovering personal preferences. All young adults examine their self-image, and most will make at least some changes based on what they're learning about themselves.

The Five W's of the College Years

Throughout college, but especially during the first year or two, students are evaluating their family's values and beliefs. Parents find that uncomfortable. As hard as it may be for you, this is work your child must do. Students are looking for the answers to five basic questions: Who? Where? What? When? Why?

- Who am I? Students are engaged in the normal process of forming an individual identity, and at the same time, determining how they fit within their family. Questioning what they've been taught is part of the process of assimilation that must occur for their values to become embedded—to make ideas and beliefs truly their own.

- Where do I belong? The college years are a time to think about how their family's social position, culture, and income influenced their upbringing. They wonder how their past will affect their future and how they can drive their own destiny.

- What will I do with my life? By the time they graduate from college, students need to have an idea about what comes next. Some students start college with a clear and unchanging vision of their future, but most are still figuring out what it means to apply their values through their work and daily actions.

- When does it all begin? When will I be grown up? Students are constantly looking toward whatever comes next—the next semester, the next stage in a relationship, or the next phase of life. They're waiting for the moment when everything will feel complete, when they will finally feel like they have "arrived." They thought it would happen when they got to college, but now they find that college is just more preparation.

- Why? The three-year-old's constant "why" reemerges in college. Students will pick apart a relationship, a plan, or their past and analyze it almost to the point of obsession. They're seeing old, familiar ideas in brand-new ways, which can be disquieting. They struggle with the idea that life is not just black and white, right or wrong, and includes many shades of gray, along with primary colors, pastels, and all kinds of tints and hues.

At some point—and maybe multiple times—you're likely to run headfirst into a major collision with your newly independent child. More than one family has seen their student come home over spring break and in short order accuse his parents of hypocrisy.

"You send a check to the Sierra Club every year, and you claim to be this major environmentalist, so why do you drive that big SUV? You seem to think that everyone else in the world should conserve energy, but you get to pollute the whole valley."

As uncomfortable as it is to have your child challenge your actions and beliefs, your explanation is important to him. In this case, your student is probably not saying you should stop sending that check to the Sierra Club, nor that you should get rid of the SUV. He probably likes driving it as much as you do, but he may genuinely be trying to make sense of how you manage to put seemingly disparate behaviors together.

Maybe you respond by admitting that you wanted a truck all your life, but you needed a family vehicle, and this was your compromise. Your son may come to see that this was a way to responsibly fulfill your fantasy without getting a full-size, four-door pickup. Or you may acknowledge that you always worried about your family's safety in your previous car, and this one had the best safety features you could find. This gives your son a glimpse of your priorities and how you work through them. He still may disagree with your rationale, but it helps to see how you reach your decisions.

Even though your child is questioning how you raised her or the things you believe in most deeply, she has heard your lessons throughout her life, and she's thinking about what you've taught her. She may not agree with everything you believe, but she will not completely reject everything she's ever learned.

Those of us who work on campus frequently hear students say, "My parents think . . ." or "My mom says . . ." or "My family always . . ." Students know their parents' opinions, and they care about their family's values and beliefs. The student who lights up her first cigarette is thinking, if not saying, "My dad would kill me if he knew I was smoking."

Every college student makes choices his parents would criticize. As the years pass, though, the mistakes and the criticisms fade. The daughter who questioned her family's religious doctrines gets married in the church where she received her First Communion or the synagogue where she had her bat mitzvah. The father and son who argued bitterly about politics end up voting for the same candidate. And sometimes parents find themselves agreeing that their child's viewpoint makes the most sense.

WHO IS THIS KID, AND WHAT DID YOU DO WITH MY *REAL* CHILD?

When parents leave their students at college, one of the great fears is that their son or daughter will change too much. They expect their child to become more mature, to grow in intellect, and to gain a focus on life. It can be hard, though, to think of all those changes happening when you aren't around.

Throughout high school, Miguel had been cynical about sports and most of the typical after-school activities. He and his friends scorned the student council members and class officers. Anything resembling school spirit irritated him. His own extracurricular activities revolved around drama club and the school plays.

At college, though, his outlook changed significantly. At his small liberal arts college, he volunteered to give tours for the admissions office and signed up for training to become an orientation leader. As a sophomore, he was elected to the undergraduate assembly, and the next year he ran for student body president. He helped organize a fun run to raise money for scholarships, and then decided he needed to train so he could do the run himself. Next he set a goal to do a half marathon.

College can bring on a complete personality reversal. Miguel's parents were impressed with all the changes they saw in him, but they couldn't help but wish they had been a part of it. It almost felt like *they* might have been the reason he was so cynical all those years. As soon as he moved away, he became energized and optimistic. It was not his family that made the difference, though. In the small-school atmosphere of Miguel's college campus—rather than the huge and highly programmed high school he had attended—he saw that his efforts could make a genuine difference.

Sometimes the changes go the other way. Dedicated academic achievers can get lost in the freedom of college life. Instructors don't take attendance, and if students don't turn in a paper, no one asks for it. There are fewer rules, and with a bit of ingenuity, most of them can be broken.

Even the most responsible college student has lapses of judgment. Your daughter gives fifty dollars to a stranger because he tells a sad story. Your son forgets his backpack on the bus and never gets it back.

The college years are a staging ground for adulthood. In most cases, mistakes are made within the relative safety of a supportive environment, and there are people around to help students pick up the pieces. Not every problem is easily remedied, unfortunately: the unplanned pregnancy, the run-in with the police after a night of drinking, or the behavior that leads to a charge of sexual assault.

When students make mistakes, their reaction might be to either dismiss it as unimportant or to give up and drop out of school rather than look for a solution. Parents, meanwhile, feel the need to step in and fix the problem. Colleges routinely hear pleas from parents saying, "He just wasn't thinking. Can't you let this go?" Whether it's underage drinking, plagiarism, or lighting a dumpster on fire after a hockey victory, families ask for leniency.

All students over the age of eighteen are adults and responsible for their actions. They should be prepared to face the consequences when they make mistakes. This, too, is part of the maturing process. Colleges, like society, enact rules and policies in order to ensure a safe and fair community for everyone who lives, works, studies, and plays on campus.

When a student breaks rules or laws, family members can sympathize but should not mediate. Telling your student you will not intervene may be the hardest thing you've ever done. It may also be the best thing you can do. When students think their parents will continue to protect them from the fallout of their actions, they never have to figure out how to fix the mistakes they've made, and they never learn to avoid future mistakes. Facing consequences is painful, but it has a purpose, and it's much better than making the same mess over and over.

QUICK TIPS FOR STUDENTS

- Because of all that you're learning from friends, instructors, and your own experience, your beliefs and values are likely to change. You might begin to question or confront your family's beliefs, rules, and priorities. If you want them to respect you and your values, do your best to respect theirs, even when you disagree.
- Know that you may soften or change your beliefs over time based on your life's experience—so may your family.
- If you have a problem—maybe you've overdrawn your bank account or you're failing chemistry—tell your

parents. Remember when you were in high school and they told you, "If you get in trouble, I want to hear it from you first"? They still feel that way.

- Don't expect your family to fix your mistakes. When you tell them what happened, have some ideas in mind about what steps you will take, and tell them that part as well.

SECTION 4
Focus on the Future

CHAPTER 12

Moving Out, Moving On

Leaving Dorm Life Behind

After the initial adjustment to college, families look forward to having some time to let things settle down. Unfortunately, the changes continue to roll in, often when they're least expected.

After Peg and Ron helped their son move into the residence hall at the beginning of his first year, they talked about all the opportunities he would have. Good grades from a prestigious university and recommendations from world-renowned professors would help him qualify for a top medical school someday. Peg and Ron would be paying back college loans for years, but it was worth it. Logan had a bright future.

Shortly after the start of his second semester, they got a Saturday afternoon phone call. Logan was yelling to be heard over the pounding bass of music in the background. "Mom! Dad! Guess what! I just got invited to pledge a fraternity, and I get to move into this amazing house with forty-two of the greatest guys I ever met!"

Today's college parents probably formed their opinions of fraternities and sororities when they were the age their student is now. Many concluded at the time that Greek life was basically an excuse for partying. Although fraternities and sororities have worked hard to upgrade their image, films and news stories continue to circulate that rowdy reputation. Sadly, hazing and the outcomes of heavy drinking, including injuries and deaths, have persistently turned public opinion against so-called Greek societies.

At their best, Greek members provide a significant service to their school and the wider community. Upperclassmen are charged with looking out for new pledges, mentoring them through the first year of college, and training them to be the leaders who will advise the next class. Philanthropy and campus involvement are requirements of membership, and Greeks often take the lead in college events like homecoming and student elections, as well as service projects—food drives, tutoring, or raising funds for charitable organizations. Members are expected to maintain a good grade point average; chapters elect an academic officer who ensures that students meet academic requirements. Their loyalty continues after graduation, as Greek alumni mentor the men and women who follow them.

At their worst, however, fraternities and sororities continue the drink-till-you-drop image. On a few campuses, neglected fraternity houses have been condemned and closed down, chapters have been banned, or the entire Greek system has been eliminated.

How does your student differentiate between the good and the bad? How can you know if the fraternity or sorority your student wants to join will be a positive or negative influence?

When Tania called home to tell her parents she wanted to pledge a sorority, they were worried. "Everyone knows about the parties and the problems," her father said. "Tania is saying this is a science and engineering group for women, and the girls are all good students. She says they'll help her when she has questions with classes like physics and calculus. Apparently, they have former members come and talk about how they found their first jobs and what they're doing now. But I'm still not happy about the whole Greek scene. It seems like trouble."

Students and parents can do their homework by researching the national organization's website. They can check the college's student organizations website to see if additional information is available on the local chapter. The student activities office should be able to say if the chapter is on probation as a student group, or if it has a positive reputation. You can ask for the chapter's grade point average and find out if information is available on the group's financial status or the condition of the house—all indicators of the chapter's character.

The best indicator of the fraternity's or sorority's character, however, is probably your own student. Greek chapters are essentially small communities; after initially meeting the students who are interested in joining, members decide who will receive an invitation. Current members want to maintain the environment they've created. They base their offers on whether a student will fit into their chapter's lifestyle and values, and they don't invite new members who will be a poor fit. If your son or daughter is a conscientious student who speaks out for social justice issues, he or she is not likely to be invited to join a group that spends Monday through Wednesday recovering from four-day weekend binges. And a student whose interests are clearly the party scene will not be asked to pledge the house that's known on campus for its community service and its no-alcohol policy.

Commuter students don't usually think about joining a fraternity or sorority, but belonging to a chapter has unique benefits for students who live off campus. Membership doesn't always require living in the house, and commuters find that by joining, they have a group of supportive friends. They also have a place to eat, socialize, and study between classes. It might even mean free parking. Plus, the commuter who decides at some point to move closer to campus has a claim on a room.

Fraternity and sorority houses can be viewed as a next step from the college residence hall. Like the dorm, students live together in a close community. The difference is that they select their own residents, and they regard one another more as family than as housemates.

The call for companionship—wanting to be with a caring group of friends—is a natural response to the upheaval of college life. A student will enroll at a large university because of all the possibilities it offers, but then wants to retreat to a homelike atmosphere with people who feel like sisters or brothers.

Still, college should be a time to learn about diversity and difference. Even if your daughter or son chooses the security of a Greek society, they should make a concerted effort to experience the opportunities and explore the medley of friendships that college offers.

FOR RENT: 2 BDRM, OFF-ST PKG, NR UNIV

At some point, you can expect to hear, "My friends and I are getting an apartment next year. We looked at some places that are just a couple of blocks from campus, and it's going to be way less expensive than the residence hall. Okay?"

Sometimes the message is more urgent. "I guess I didn't tell you. I missed the reapplication deadline to live in the dorm next year, so I don't have anyplace to live. There's a guy I found online who needs a roommate for fall semester, and I'm on my way to take a look at his place."

For commuter students, any announcement about moving into an apartment is accompanied by a calculation of the hours they will save by living closer to campus, the money saved in gas or bus fares, and the academic benefits of living closer to the chemistry lab.

Families might first hear about an apartment after winter

break during the freshman or sophomore year, but increasingly the announcement comes just a few weeks after moving their first-year student to campus and long before parents are ready for it. "The best apartments go fast, so I have to sign a lease before the end of October. Me and my friends found a place we love. I'm sending photos."

At that point, parents have barely begun to feel like the first year of college might actually turn out all right. They believe their student has plenty of independence, with guidance comfortably nearby when it's needed. For commuter students living at home, curfews and chore assignments have been relaxed to accommodate student life. How much more freedom does a student need?

Thinking about an apartment, parents once again revert to worries about safety and their child's ability to take care of himself. They question the financial advantages—is it really going to save any money? Discussions become all the more complicated when lease confirmation requires first and last month's rent plus a hefty damage deposit. Your student is asking you to hand over money that was not in your budget. Your reaction is, "If you think you're ready for an apartment, maybe you should come up with the deposit yourself."

From a developmental standpoint, apartment living is a natural next step from residence halls. Students learn to share responsibilities, identify priorities, and manage a shared household in a relatively safe environment. These are all skills that will transfer to intimate relationships, marriage, and the world of work. The presence of roommates continues the supportive atmosphere of the residence halls. Young adults can work through life's challenges in partnership with friends who are going through the same experiences.

An apartment represents independence, but not every student is ready for an apartment at the beginning of the sophomore year, or for that matter, during their junior year. The steps from dependence to responsibility are predictable, but they don't always fall in a straight line. If this is the first you've heard about an apartment, you may have cause for worry. Moving into an apartment should not be a snap decision. Peer pressure can cause students to link up with roommates they hardly know and may not even *like* six months from now.

Your son or daughter is convinced that everything will work out, but you want to feel comfortable about this decision, too. There are some obvious clues to indicate whether your child is ready for an apartment:

- *During the past year, has your student made good choices?* Are you confident that she can manage her finances? Are you comfortable with the friends she has made? Has she demonstrated that she can balance social, personal, and academic demands?
- *Ask why she wants to live off campus.* Most students say they can save money by living off campus. Rent costs may sound less expensive than room and board in the residence hall, but be sure the full budget picture includes groceries, transportation to classes, utilities, and parking.
- *Are the budget estimates reasonable?* In most college communities, on- and off-campus expenses tend to be comparable on a monthly basis, but an apartment might mean a twelve-month commitment. That can mean an extra few thousand dollars.

Students who say they will study better in an apartment, or they can't bear the noise in the residence hall, might be surprised to find that life is no better when they live off campus. If, however, your child convinces you that he is realistic about the responsibilities and ready for an apartment, he probably is ready for this next step in the growing-up process.

Although the best preparations cannot prevent every problem, it's a good idea to have a conversation about apartments long before your student is ready to sign a lease. During holiday or summer breaks, parents and students should be talking about when an apartment makes sense and what general guidelines you require. Maybe you don't want your student living on the ground floor in a building with no security entrance; perhaps you want your child to live within walking distance of campus since he will not have a car. And you can ask your student to demonstrate apartment-readiness by buying groceries on a budget, fixing a few meals, and cleaning the bathroom at home during breaks.

If you still find yourself worrying about your student leaving the protection of the residence hall, think about your underlying concerns and whether they're realistic:

- *It's too much responsibility. She needs to focus on studying.* If your child has developed good study habits, she will probably maintain them wherever she is living.
- *She won't eat well.* Let her know this is a concern, and ask what she and her roommates are planning to do about meals. You *should* be concerned if she says, "There's a taco shop on the ground floor of the building. We figure we can always run downstairs and pick up something." On the other hand, you can stop worrying if you know your student can cook and has prepared meals at home. Maybe she has decided to sign up for a once-a-day meal plan at the dining center, or she may be planning to apply for a food service job

that would allow her to eat on campus. If your student has done some thoughtful planning about food, she'll be fine.

- *I'm worried about sex. I think he's getting an apartment so he can have his girlfriend over.* If students want to have sex, they will. An apartment might provide more privacy, but living arrangements are not a deciding factor in whether students have sex.

- *I've heard about "house parties." I don't want to pay all that money for an apartment just so he can have drinking parties every weekend.* Like the sex issue, students who want to party will find a way. Most students will want to host the occasional party. At least some of the charm of having your own place is showing it off to friends, but responsible students are not going to risk their damage deposit or invite the possibility of eviction by letting things get out of control. You have reason to worry if your student rents an apartment in a building with a reputation for noise and drinking. The rental across the street from the football stadium or the run-down house in the block behind fraternity row might be a poor choice. If you know that your child routinely drinks too much on weekends, and he chooses a place that already reeks of stale beer, an apartment will not help him become a better scholar.

Most colleges and universities offer apartment-style campus housing as an alternative to traditional residence halls. Studios and one- or two-bedroom suites, located on campus and managed by university housing staff, provide the floor plan and self-sufficiency of independent living. Students are still subject to campus policies and supervision. Campus apartments can offer a smooth transition out of a dorm into more independent living.

At the age of eighteen, students are legally able to sign an apartment lease on their own, but it's a good idea for parents to review the paperwork or even see the apartment before the student finalizes an agreement. Seeing an apartment is not always a possibility for out-of-town parents, but the more you know about the lease, the apartment, and the roommates, the more comfortable you will feel.

A point to consider: when an apartment will be housing four, five, or more roommates, the "helpful advice" of anywhere from four to ten parents is way too much.

PREREQUISITES FOR APARTMENT LIVING

When students move into their first apartment, a whole new set of skills are required, including paying bills on time. Even if parents continue to support their students, the bills will be in the students' names and will go to their address. Before signing a joint lease with friends, students need to talk about what that will mean to each roommate:

- *How much can they afford?* Roommates will have to agree on how much rent they can pay. Within a residence hall, everyone shares the same basic living conditions, and socioeconomic differences may not be noticeable. A student from a wealthy family, however, might expect to move into a luxury apartment across the street from the recreation center, while her best friend can only afford the upstairs of a house eight blocks away.
- *What amenities matter?* Are roommates willing to share a bedroom? How many people will be using a bathroom? How important are in-apartment washers, dryers, dishwashers, and other appliances?

- *What transportation issues might arise?* Will one or more of the roommates have a car? If only one student has a car, can roommates use it? If more than one person has a car, who gets the reserved parking space?
- *Are all the roommates equally committed to the rental agreement?* When they sign a lease, they are responsible to fulfill certain requirements. Depending on state laws, local ordinances, or the preference of the landlord, that responsibility may be jointly connected to all tenants; if one roommate fails to pay the rent, all could be evicted. Sometimes only one student signs the lease and writes the check, and that student must trust the others to hand over their share. Some landlords require parents to cosign the lease and take responsibility for any unpaid charges. Tenants are required to maintain a respectable level of cleanliness and behavior. If police are called for loud parties, the lease could be canceled, or the rent could be raised. Students can't just walk away from a lease. If a student decides next week to live with other friends or drops out of school, who is responsible for that portion of the rent?

Even the best-prepared roommates might find that apartment living delivers some major disappointments. The rose-tinted image is that having your own space will mean time spent fussing over gourmet meals, relaxing together on the balcony, or—in the more upscale student apartments—working out in the building's fitness studio or hanging out by the infinity pool.

The reality is that cooking and cleaning take time and require roommate concessions. Before committing to a lease, they should talk about how they will divide chores. Some students are great cooks, some are meticulous housekeepers, and some are willing to do the real dirty work. Others turn out to be pretty much useless.

Emily volunteered to be the cook in her apartment. With no classes scheduled after 3:00 p.m., she offered to fix dinners for her roommates, and she promised to have meals on the table at 6:30 each night. In return Dina was willing to wash dishes and clean the kitchen after dinner, and Tammy said she would be responsible for cleaning the rest of the apartment on weekends. Within a few weeks, however, it was clear that things were not working out. Tammy came home hungry at 4:30 every afternoon and raided the refrigerator, so she wasn't interested in dinner. Dina didn't see the sense of running the dishwasher every night, and once or twice a week was often enough to clean the kitchen.

Before long, Emily declared she was done cooking. "With all these pots and pans sitting in the sink, I have to wash them before I can make anything. Tammy doesn't eat dinner, but she's in my way when I'm trying to cook. It's just not working. Let's all buy our own groceries and fix our own meals."

The work involved with housekeeping, along with the inevitable roommate conflicts, takes its toll. Grades suffer when students move into their first apartment. But after the initial glow and high expectations of apartment life has passed, homemaking and academics become better integrated. Roommates work out an acceptable division of labor, and when they come home from class, they carve out time to study. Most students end up fending for themselves—when they're hungry, they open the cupboard and grab whatever takes the least effort to prepare. Standard fare for the college diet is pasta with ready-made sauce or rice topped by a can of soup and accompanied by half a bag of salad. Tacos, spaghetti, and gourmet peanut butter and jelly sandwiches are about as fancy as it gets, and the grocery store deli becomes a daily destination.

FRIENDS, ROOMMATES, OR LOVERS?

"One male or female roommate wanted, nonsmoker, to share two-bedroom apartment near campus."

Mixing genders in an apartment feels inappropriate to most parents. How can college-aged students *not* become involved when they're living together? Even the most platonic intentions are too easily set aside when twenty-year-olds share a bathroom and sleep in adjoining rooms—or share a bedroom. As long as parents are paying the rent, they can set a few limits, and many parents insist that their student live with others of the same gender.

Still, it can work well to have men and women share an apartment, as long as they approach the arrangement with a sense of reality and clear ground rules. Most students spend their freshman year in a mixed-gender residence hall. They shuffle to breakfast together wearing baggy sweatpants and slippers, without benefit of makeup or a shower. It's not a big step to a nonsexual relationship in a shared apartment. When they select their first apartment, students tend to pick friends, not lovers.

Moving in with a romantic partner is a step that most young adults approach cautiously. Living together represents a commitment. Students know that a breakup can leave them with serious decisions about what happens next and where they will live. While students might select roommates in a relatively nonchalant manner, figuring that it's only for a year, they don't savor the prospect of living with an ex if the relationship goes bad.

APARTMENTS: THE GOOD, THE BAD, AND THE REALLY UGLY

The standards of student apartments vary immensely, ranging from old houses that have seen decades of use and abuse by college students to ultraluxury high-rise apartments with built-in washers and dryers, separate bedroom-bath suites for each roommate, and a makerspace with high-end 3-D printers next to the concierge desk in the lobby. Quartz countertops in the kitchen, queen-size lofted beds in the bedroom, a gas fireplace in the living room, and a rooftop deck with a fire pit might be more than most students will be able to afford after they graduate, but the bar has been set by their college housing.

Wherever students choose to live, a first step when they move in is to mark their territory as their own. Parents tread carefully when they venture into their child's apartment. When you visit, do you ignore the obvious problems or make the obvious suggestions?

Phoebe refused all offers of help when she moved into her first apartment, saying that she didn't want her mother to see it until she and her roommates had settled in. Two weeks later, she called and invited her mother to come for dinner. "I can't wait for you to see what we've done. We hung some pictures, and we bought a coffee table. I even got some new blinds for the kitchen. You'll love it."

As hard as her mother tried to focus on the decorating, she couldn't ignore the stained sofa in the living room, the dangling light fixture in the hallway, and the constant drip of the kitchen faucet. "You've done a great job here," she told Phoebe midway through dinner. "I love the blinds, and the coffee table is a nice touch. I think, though, that the landlord needs to hear about that faucet and the hall light. And can you find out if they can replace the sofa? It's pretty bad."

"Mom, we can't complain! Do you know how lucky we were to get this place? We want to live here next year, too, so we can't have the landlord thinking we're high maintenance."

Students learn valuable lessons by living on their own, including what legal rights they have and how to negotiate repairs and other tenant issues. Many young men and women have never before had to assert their rights without assistance or coaching, and they may not be prepared for the unexpected events that are sure to come up. One student called her father late at night, nearly hysterical. "Dad, I saw a mouse in the hallway! Right outside my door! What are we supposed to do? It's gross!"

"It's not the end of the world," he assured her. "No, you don't want mice in your apartment, but it's not going to actually hurt you. In the morning, call the apartment manager. They'll put out a trap or some poison. And the important thing is that you need to keep your apartment clean and make sure there's not any food that mice can get into."

Most students face at least a few problems as they learn to cope with the world of leases, landlords, and independent living. They will still want their parents' advice and the occasional helping hand. They'll send a text message from the grocery store to find out what ingredients they need to make your famous omelet. Or they'll give you a call Saturday afternoon to let you know, "I bought a bookcase on sale today, but it's all in pieces. Can you maybe come up tomorrow and put it together?"

Your help—and any duplicate cookware, tools, or patio furniture you might have lying around—will be happily received. Your son or daughter will be grateful for a gift box of packaged foods in the mail or the occasional bag of groceries when you come to visit.

A twelve-month apartment lease most likely means your child will no longer come home for the summer. Although most students go home the summer after their first year, the numbers taper off after the sophomore year. By the time they have their own apartment, students feel that their home is on campus. As one second-year student tactlessly told her mother, "There's really nothing for me at home anymore." Even if you live only a twenty-minute drive away, and even if your student comes home every weekend to do his laundry and raid your refrigerator, having an apartment means he's moved out. Your child still needs you, just not in the same ways.

QUICK TIPS FOR STUDENTS

- If you go through fraternity or sorority rush, be yourself. Greek chapters are looking for pledges who will fit into the culture of their house. If they don't see the real you, you could be setting yourself up for a miserable match.
- Moving into an apartment is a natural progression from residence hall living, but it calls for more responsibility. Do some solid research before committing to a lease, and be sure you know what is included in the rent, as well as what extra expenses you'll be paying. Are utilities (water, heat, and electricity) included in the monthly cost? If you're going to have a car, is there a parking space? Does parking cost extra?
- Consider the up-front costs of an apartment. If you have to pay first and last months' rent and a damage deposit in order to confirm the lease, do you have that lump sum on hand? Do your roommates have funds for the rent and damage deposit?
- If anything seems unclear about the arrangements you're making, the apartment you're planning to live in, or the terms of the lease, ask for time to think it over. You should be able to see the exact apartment you will be renting, and the lease should stipulate the rental amount for the entire length of the contract. Be cautious if there are stipulations for the rent to

be raised at the discretion of the manager. In some leases, a single noise complaint could increase your rent or even be grounds for eviction.

- If your college has a student legal services office, ask them to review your lease before you sign it. If you have a dispute with your landlord, take your lease and your complaint to the student legal services office to see if they can help.

- Talk with your roommates about how you'll handle bill paying, how you'll divide housework, and how you'll deal with disagreements.

- Practice your housekeeping skills. Make sure you know how to cook, clean, and take care of minor household repairs. Hint: your parents will be much more receptive to the idea of an apartment if you offer to do these tasks at home *before* you mention that you want to move out of the dorm.

CHAPTER 13

What Can You Do with a Sociology Degree?

Choosing a Life and *a Job*

Every now and then, you notice people who are obviously enjoying their work—the gardener at the botanical gardens, the chef at the sushi bar—and you think, "I'd like that job. It looks like fun."

Students face these temptations every day. Colleges spread out a smorgasbord of academic appetizers and invite students to sample a little of everything. With each class they take, they're making judgments, deciding they want to delve deeper into one subject area or vowing they will never take a second course in another.

The developmental processes of young adults are also part of the picture. College students are examining their values and exploring new interests. One of the most exciting outcomes of a good class schedule is the occasional "Eureka!" moment when everything comes together. The poem a student is reading for English class portrays the same event as a painting in last year's art history textbook, and it perfectly illustrates this week's lecture in Psychology of Religion and all those stories Grandma tells about her childhood in Georgia.

Families want their students to genuinely enjoy the process of learning, but the ultimate goal of a successful college career is not whether students have fun in their classes. When they walk offstage on graduation day, the hope for these new grads is that they'll be that mature, responsible adult we've all been waiting for. In a perfect world, they would have a professional job starting within a few days; it would pay a livable wage, and they would live happily ever after. Families would be willing to defer those goals if graduate school would qualify their student for a better career and an even better life in a couple of years.

THE CHANGING MIND

Most students start college with at least a vague idea of their future. Career plans, however, can change, sometimes for the most unexpected reasons. A student might take a course because it's required, but he finds it's a subject that simply makes sense to him. An instructor who loves his subject can bring a lecture to life and draw a student into a field of study.

Matt, who was "kind of thinking about a psychology major and then maybe forensic science," signed up for a geology course his second semester. He liked the schedule—classes met in the middle of the day, so no early morning or night classes—and it would fulfill his natural science requirement. Although much of the coursework centered on tectonics, glaciers, and rock and mineral identification, Matt was fascinated by the professor's stories about his fieldwork and research. "This guy can make *rocks* interesting! One day he talked about studies he's done on coral reefs—how changes in rock temperature and water currents affect the reefs. I was actually disappointed when the class ended. I could have listened to him for hours. I would love to know a subject like he does."

The next year, Matt took another course from the same professor, and the following summer he applied for a part-time job in the geology department. Eventually, he decided to go to graduate school to study hydrogeology, a subject he never knew existed until he stumbled upon that first geology class.

RETHINKING THE LIFE PLAN

Sometimes students come face-to-face with the reality that they picked the wrong major. If they discover they're bored or disillusioned by the classes they're required to take for their field of study, they face a tremendous letdown. Worse, they may find they don't qualify for the major they dreamed of, or that they simply can't work in that field. The student who planned to be a veterinarian will be forced to rethink her goals if she can't pass organic chemistry or if she develops an allergy to animal dander.

The most common reason for switching majors, though, is that *students* change. The careful, conservative sophomore who settled on a "safe" choice when he started college now recognizes that he excels in his classes, and he doesn't need to limit himself. His wild-eyed, unfocused roommate discovers a subject he loves and becomes focused. Education at its best opens students to new possibilities and inspires them to expand their vision.

Any students who are reexamining career goals have a lot to think about, and they agonize over the decision. Changing majors can mean that a few or maybe even all of the classes they've taken don't count toward the new major. They may have to transfer to another university that offers the degree they want.

Sometimes parents are not so much disappointed as surprised. They don't hear about the new direction until a decision has been made, and they can't understand the thought process their student has gone through. As a parent, you can hardly help but question the decision. "Are you sure? Have you talked to anyone about this? *Why?*"

Most students refine and refocus their life plans at least somewhat during college. A change from journalism to technical writing might seem like a smart, strategic move, but it's much harder to understand the change from business administration to gender studies. A father complained that his son wanted to switch from the engineering department to education. "He hasn't really thought this through. I think he's just listening to his friends. They're all English and history majors, and their classes are easier. But I don't think my son realizes how much less he would earn as a teacher. I'm afraid he's throwing away his future."

PASSION OR PRACTICALITY?

A long list of motivational speakers make their living by encouraging college students to find their passion. "Do what you love, and you'll never work a day in your life." Nothing makes the college experience more exciting for students than studying a topic that energizes them. But passion doesn't always translate into a paycheck. For every student who majors in theater and goes on to a successful acting career, there are many more who don't. The archaeology major who dreams of discovering ancient Roman artifacts may never end up doing fieldwork. That doesn't mean they don't find jobs they love or find ways to bring their major into their daily life.

Researchers have found that when eighteen-year-old college students declare their passion and focus their pursuits on that one area, they actually may be limiting themselves by failing to explore other possibilities. They cut off the potential of discovering something they might love even more. Passion for a subject can fade over time, and the reality of creating a life around that one bright flame might eventually burn out. If things don't work out in the area they've been pursuing, they don't have other interests to turn to. Rather than "follow your passion," a better recommendation is *"develop* your passion."[22] By all means, students should make room for what is meaningful and important, but they need to be open to what else excites them as well.

A CHANGING ECONOMY MEANS AN UNCERTAIN FUTURE

The job a student prepares for today might well be outmoded before the job search begins. Print journalism is already a disappearing profession. As libraries put their resources into technology rather than books, and online searches take over the role of research specialists, the demand for librarians is declining. Software has reduced the need for bookkeepers, accountants, and even lawyers, as programs and apps calculate data according to a formula, and anyone can use a template to fill in legal documents. As businesses merge and companies become larger, fewer middle management positions will be needed. Jobs in health care, education, social services, and customer/client services will still need workers, but how those jobs are done will change.

Career planning in a gig economy means developing skills that can translate to multiple professions over a lifetime and an ever-changing landscape. Future employment will require a blend of characteristics and talents, and the predicted list includes:

- Critical thinking and problem solving
- Verbal and written communication
- Teamwork and collaboration
- Digital technology aptitude
- Leadership

---

22. P. A. O'Keefe, C. S. Dweck, and G. M. Walton, "Implicit Theories of Interest: Finding Your Passion or Developing It?" http://gregorywalton-stanford.weebly.com/uploads/4/9/4/4/49448111/okeefedweckwalton_2018.pdf.

- Global and intercultural fluency
- Innovation and creativity[23]

For some graduates, the first job after college will not mean a traditional, entry-level position, with a nine-to-five schedule and a cubicle workspace. Instead it might look like a patchwork quilt. A "portfolio career" can stitch together a combination of part-time positions, freelance work, and temporary jobs built around an individual's skills, interests, and the need to pay their bills. Work might be done online or conducted in shared or coworker office space or at home. While plenty of traditional jobs will remain, a rising wave of job opportunities will rely on businesses identifying a specific problem to be solved and finding the person who will contract to do that piece of work.

As routine tasks are increasingly given over to machines, employees will do the jobs that robots cannot. College students today have developed digital literacy throughout their lives, and they are becoming the human interface for artificial intelligence. Their employment will not necessarily rely on performing the digital and technical tasks, but on being able to predict and plan complex solutions. They will need verbal, written, and presentation skills to communicate intricate information. And all those entrepreneurs managing their own careers will need to understand marketing, time management, budgeting, and the tax system.

STRATEGIC CAREER PLANNING

As Sandra's son, Seth, began his last year of college, she asked if he had thought about starting a job hunt yet. "No, not yet. I can't

23. NACE, "Career Readiness Defined," https://www.naceweb.org/career -readiness/competencies/career-readiness-defined/.

apply for jobs now, can I?" he asked. "It will be next summer before I can start working."

"My boss's son had a job offer months before he graduated," Sandra said. "I think there are some steps you should be taking now."

In fact, Seth should have been taking some steps all along. Colleges and universities offer help with career development and planning, beginning in the freshman year.

Step 1: Self-exploration. First-year students are naturally engaged in identifying their personal values, interests, skills, and abilities—the very information they will need to know in order to lay the foundation for a career. Whether or not they're ready to select a specific major or future profession, most young adults have some sense of how they want to spend their lives. Are they most comfortable with a daily routine, or do they need constant challenge and stimulation? What personal talents and abilities can they draw on? Most colleges provide online or in-person classes and workshops to help students explore how their skills and interests fit with different careers.

Career advisers can administer tests that help students understand their personality traits and consider how those characteristics relate to different professions. For example, introverts probably won't be happy in a position that requires them to meet the public all day, every day. Someone who appreciates order and routine will not want a job with constant change and surprises.

Step 2: Information gathering. In this step, students are looking for guidance on what they need to do, what they should learn, and how long it will take to qualify for the kind of work they are considering. The student who wants to be a lawyer will have to consider not only the demands of the coursework, but also the finances to pay for law school and the stamina for three more years of education following an undergraduate degree. The potential concert violinist must face the daunting question of whether she has the talent and perseverance to prepare for such a competitive field.

During this phase of career investigation, an academic adviser can help define majors and credentials that relate to the profession the student is considering. Career advisers can identify skills that will be beneficial for the position and different paths to get there. A student who is interested in a corporate career might think his only academic option is the college's business school. Depending on the kind of job, though, students may be better prepared by studying economics in the liberal arts college, marketing in the communication department, or agricultural business in a department of agriculture.

Advisers also can help students set up informational interviews with people working in the field who can talk about the real-world experience of the job. They can identify the skills that have helped them the most or discuss what they wish they had known when they first started in the profession. The more students know about the career they're considering, the better they can prepare for it.

By the end of their second year of college, students should have some sense of a general career area that most interests them. This is a significant step for students, but it can lead to surprises or disappointments for parents who had their own ideas about their child's future profession. Parents, like their students, need to keep an open mind about the possibilities. The jobs that students end up with are often not obvious based on the major. Sociology graduates find jobs in business, human services, criminal justice, social work, and government. A history degree can lead to museum work, diplomatic service, tourism, grant writing, or business management.

Step 3: Limiting step. During the junior and senior years, students take more classes in their area of study. In the limiting step, students begin to understand the different facets of a major and narrow their focus to the specialty that most interests them. A student whose major is human development takes a class on family relationships to prepare herself for working with families of children with disabilities. The student sitting next to her in class is planning to work with adoptive parents, and a student in the front row hopes to do research on multigenerational families for public policy development.

Some students might still have multiple career options in mind, and they're not ready to give up on any of them yet. "I really love biology, but I think I might want to be a lawyer some-day. Since most pre-law students get a degree in political science, I'm wondering if I should change my major to poli sci."

Not only might a minor or a second major be the answer to combining multiple interests into a satisfying career, but it also could provide a way to distinguish a student from all the other job or grad school applicants. The aspiring attorney learns that law school admissions committees see a biology degree with a political science minor as great preparation for a future in envi-ronmental law.

Parents help in this stage by encouraging students to take advantage of the full range of career exploration opportunities and to take note of the people they're meeting. On her father's suggestion, Regina diligently recorded the names of every pro-fessional she came across—guest lecturers in her communication courses, speakers who addressed her communication club, and anyone she met when she toured her mentor's workplace. When the time came to look for an internship, she sent messages to everyone on her list, asking for advice. "I'm sure most of them didn't remember who I was," she said. "But it worked. I actu-ally got two internships—a semester-long internship at a news bureau here in town and a summer position at the Democratic headquarters in Washington, D.C."

Step 4: The employment step. This stage encompasses the serious work of getting an internship and a job. It starts with developing skills for the job hunt and continues through the process of landing a position. It includes preparing a résumé, writing cover letters, making follow-up phone calls, and interviewing for positions. If students wait until graduation to begin these groundwork tasks, they will lose the advantage to job applicants who have done the preparation.

INTERNSHIPS: REAL-WORLD EXPERIENCE!

A typical entry-level job posting is likely to look something like this: *Recreation Coordinator position: Qualifications include graduation from an accredited college or university with a bachelor's degree and coursework in recreation or a related field. One year full-time experience required, involving the planning, promotion, development, and supervision of recreation programs for all ages.*

Therein lies the catch-22 of the job market: You can't get a job without having work history, and you can't get work history without a job. The answer to the problem is internships, those short-term (and often unpaid) positions that give students a chance to put their classroom knowledge to work under the supervision of a practicing professional. Internships have become almost a requirement for upperclassmen. The "demonstrated knowledge" or "previous experience" that employers demand as preparation for an entry-level position must come from somewhere, and students are combining multiple internships to demonstrate that they meet the requirements. Students struggle, though, to fit another obligation into their academic schedule, and it's especially challenging when the internship is unpaid and must be squeezed in among class, study, and paid employment hours.

As internships have become a necessary step in career preparation, they have become increasingly competitive. Landing an internship—even an unpaid position—with a Fortune 500 company seems like a coup. When it comes time to apply for a professional position, however, students need to document what they learned in their internship. A three-month stint of unskilled tasks like filing or running errands, even at a major firm, is less useful in the job hunt than a position at a less prestigious company where the student was able to build a website or staff a team that wrote a five-year marketing plan.

Internships are not the only way for students to gain experience that provides job preparation. Volunteer programs offer many of the practical experiences that internships do. Part-time jobs, often on campus, teach competencies that students will use in a full-time position. Learning abroad programs give students practice in problem solving and innovation, and some include internships, volunteer opportunities, or research experience.

Parents can be helpful in the search for internships by encouraging their student to identify the following:

- What kind of work will the student be doing on the job, during the internship, or in the volunteer position?
- What will the student learn?
- Does this experience provide credits toward graduation? Some internship and research programs allow students to earn academic credits through a career exploration course. Study abroad experiences through the college or university can be connected to the course curriculum.
- How will this help toward qualifying for a job in the future? Is that future job one that the student really wants?

- If it is an unpaid internship or research project, is there a chance it might lead to a paid internship or a job?

LOOKING FOR WORK IN ALL THE RIGHT PLACES

When recruiters come to campus and schedule employment interviews, students in business, engineering, or other technical fields might find themselves in high demand. Meanwhile, students majoring in English, history, philosophy, and psychology read through the job notices and decide that their job hunt is hopeless. Although students have heard for years that a liberal arts background is the best possible preparation for a well-rounded employee, they grow discouraged as they look at job listings that ask for specialized training or technical skills—qualifications they do not have. Liberal arts students *do* have a solid background for any number of jobs, but they have to be prepared to explain why they are the ideal candidate. That requires reflection, preparation, and persuasion.

With graduation on the horizon, students can check in with the career office on campus for guidance on sorting through job announcements and ideas on responding to them. Workshops about résumé writing, cover letters, and interview techniques give students the tools and the confidence they need to navigate a job search. They can learn how to research companies to determine if they will fit into the corporate or organizational culture. They also can use that research to modify their résumé and cover letter to best illustrate how they meet the requirements of the position.

Campus career offices are likely to have job boards with announcements of job postings. Advisers will be able to suggest career fairs and let students know when companies will have recruiters on campus. Through online job search sites, students can send their résumé to literally hundreds of companies at once. While these websites may not be the most effective way to search, they might be the most efficient. Applicants upload a cover letter and résumé, which are evaluated by scanning for keywords that match job descriptions. Hundreds of applicants might apply for a single position, but an applicant can get her name in front of dozens of employers with a single upload.

The online search should not be the sole focus. Even in a technological world, most jobs go to applicants who make personal contact or who are recommended by a current employee or trusted colleague. Networking works.

SELLING ONESELF

College students accomplish amazing achievements through the things they do every day on and around campus. A volunteer for Habitat for Humanity joins forces with members of the community to rehabilitate a home. In the process, he gets experience not only in carpentry, plumbing, laying carpet, and grouting tile, but also in team building, project management, design, problem solving, and conflict resolution. A sorority organizes a food shelf drive and learns about event planning, marketing, and customer service. Six friends recognize that transfer students need support when they start at a new university, and they draft bylaws and establish a new student group. They learn about organizational structure, budget management, and parliamentary procedure.

Unfortunately, students seldom recognize the career and life skills they gain from their club activities and community service. By the time students are ready to graduate, they've forgotten the accomplishments they made a year or two earlier, and they fail to see the progress they've made over their college career. Even as a first-year student, it makes sense to set aside a bit of time each semester to document involvement and accomplishments. A résumé for an internship, a scholarship application, or a professional position after college should not be just a list of memberships and jobs, but also illustrations of the skills students have learned and the contributions they've made.

MY PARENTS SPENT $100,000 ON COLLEGE, AND YOU'RE OFFERING ME A SALARY OF *WHAT?*

Students start their college career thinking they're on the fast track to a high-paying job, and they will be millionaires by the time they're twenty-five. The reports are legendary of college graduates—or dropouts—who developed a start-up company that grew to be worth a hundred million dollars. Every student has heard of someone who figured out how to make a fortune with a clever idea or won a jackpot playing online poker. When students catch on that their first job is not likely to provide the dream lifestyle they were expecting—at least not right away— they wonder, "What's wrong with this system?"

It's not only the salary that's discouraging. The time and effort involved with a job search feels like full-time work with no pay. The concept that a job search is likely to take five or six months simply doesn't compute. Coming from a generation that's accustomed to instant answers, students are discouraged to learn that a job interview today doesn't yield an offer tomorrow. When they follow up with the employer and hear that the company is still conducting interviews or is seeking hiring approval from the executive office, they decide to jump right into graduate school in order to qualify for a better position in two or three years.

Parents, advisers, and faculty frequently have a better long-term view than the student when it comes to developing career strategies and time lines. Faced with a job offer that pays less than expected, students may need a reminder that working for a nonprofit organization will be good experience for a better-paying corporate position in a year or two. Or it makes sense when a professor recommends working for a couple of years before starting graduate school.

Unfortunately, the future doesn't always present itself on a prescribed schedule. For a large percentage of students, commencement day brings conflicting emotions—they're done with college, but they have nothing scheduled on the calendar for tomorrow.

Neither the student nor his parents should panic if that first professional job is not secured by graduation. Waiting tables, driving a ride share, or taking a temporary job working for a friend's dad are not the worst options for students for a few months. A job applicant needs to have some money coming in, but he also needs flexibility for scheduling interviews. The credentials are in hand, and a job will come with persistence. Positions open up throughout the summer and on into fall.

Temporary jobs and part-time positions may not be what you and your student planned for postcollege life, but they can lead to career-path jobs. Teaching an exercise course at the YMCA, doing research for a professor's grant project, or working on an election campaign all provide transferable skills. The Peace Corps, AmeriCorps, and Teach For America experiences are valuable transition options, giving students experience as well as a chance to focus on career direction. As an added bonus, some of these volunteer positions can reduce the amount students must repay on their student loans.

Whether or not there's a job waiting as soon as your student steps off the stage at graduation, you're both headed for yet another transition.

QUICK TIPS FOR STUDENTS

- You will change a lot during your four years in college. Don't feel that you have to stick to the career goal you declared as a first-year student. If one of your classes seems especially interesting, or if you learn about an intriguing job, allow yourself to think about a different path.

- Talk to your counselor or adviser at least once each year. Not only do advisers keep students on track for graduation, but they also have good tips for thinking about career preparation.

- Take advantage of mentor programs, job shadowing, and networking opportunities. People who are working in a field that interests you can tell you what the job is really like.

- When you apply for internships, look for a position that will allow opportunities for on-the-job observations and hands-on experiences, not just busy work.

- Talk to the professors in your major. They know the field and the kind of jobs their former students have taken. They can predict how the profession is likely to change in the near future. They can also write letters of recommendation that will support your job or graduate school applications.

CHAPTER 14

I'll *Always* Be Here
If You Need Me

Mentoring for a Lifetime

The last few months of college raise a whole new set of concerns for parents. While most students are clearly moving toward their postcollege plans, a number of parents are seeing few signs of progress in their students, and plenty of indications of backsliding. The hands-off parenting methods they had finally mastered now seem all wrong. The self-confidence they saw in their sons or daughters a year ago is evaporating, replaced by a curious combination of frenzied excitement and cold fear: "I'm done with college!"

When their children were graduating from high school, family members were involved in the entire process. At the transition out of college, the family role is much less clear. Students, who have made all kinds of decisions on their own during the past few years, now worry that every choice seems so much more significant. They're faced with options that could take them in very different directions, any of which could lead to raging success or dashing failure, and they would be happy to turn the decision making over to someone else.

Students need respectful support at this stage more than

they need a parent's advice. When you offer your opinion on your son's or daughter's career decisions, you have three strikes against you:

- *You don't know all the details, so you can't make a fully informed recommendation.* If your student is weighing two job possibilities, the company offering a better salary might seem like the obvious choice to you. However, a highly supportive supervisor, great benefits, or better chances for advancement could make the lower-paying job the best option in the long run.
- *You might be too emotionally involved to offer an unbiased opinion.* An opportunity that will bring your student closer to home may seem more appealing to you than the position halfway across the country. Or maybe you can think of a lot of reasons to visit your son several times a year if he takes a job in Alexandria, Virginia. But Alexandria, Louisiana?
- *If your student heeds your advice and something goes wrong, you will feel responsible.*

As important as a first professional job is, it is not a lifelong commitment. It's a first step and a trial run. Just as students were advised to build their résumé during their college years, they are now counseled to develop skills and add credentials at the start of their career. It's tempting, and even logical, to pay more attention to professional development opportunities in the first job than to focus on finances. As one recent graduate explained to her mother, "Mom, you need to understand something about our generation. We don't take just any job after graduation. I only want a job on my résumé that will get me where I want to go."

Still, graduates need a livable income. At this point, it's more helpful to give your student some questions to consider rather than offer unsolicited advice. Ask your student to think about the following:

- Will the salary cover housing and other expenses in the community where the job is located?
- If the student needs to make loan payments and buy a car, is the salary sufficient for all the bills?
- If the job requires a long-distance move, are moving expenses covered?
- How long does the student expect to stay in the position? Does the job offer opportunities to advance within the organization, or is it a stepping-stone to something else?
- What benefits does the company offer?

Parents cannot—and should not be tempted to—negotiate their child's job offer. You *can* play a coaching or mentoring role as your son or daughter weighs a proposal. A recent graduate might never have thought about various types of insurance plans, paid time off, or retirement investments, and a job offer can force them to learn quickly.

After Hannah was offered a job in Baltimore, she called her father to tell him the good news. "Dad, they offered me the job! The salary is pretty close to what I was hoping for. And don't worry, I asked and they said I can get health insurance. I'm going to take the weekend to think it over, but I'm pretty sure this is what I want."

A day later, Hannah called back to ask for help. "They have a website with their benefits package, and they said to look it over. It's really confusing. I'm supposed to choose from a menu of health care coverage and benefits. There's a health savings account, a group health plan with different deductibles, something about retirement that I can contribute to. They'll match some amount toward retirement, but that doesn't kick in for two years. There are a lot of decisions, and it's going to make a difference in how much pay I end up with every month. Can I send you the link to the website so you can talk this through with me?"

Hannah's father worked with her to determine a few different scenarios—one that would keep her monthly paycheck higher by selecting the basic health insurance and retirement plans; another option would lower her income now but pay for more of the monthly medical prescriptions she needed; and a third choice would draw down her take-home pay still more—maybe too much—but build up a good retirement fund. Hannah chose the middle route, deciding that she would come out ahead because of her prescriptions, even though it meant she would contribute less to retirement. Because she didn't plan on staying in Baltimore more than a year or two, she would save what she could for now and negotiate for a good retirement plan in her next job.

In the meantime, though, her father suggested several more questions for her to consider. "You don't need to talk about this with the person who's offering you the job, Hannah, but call the human resources department on Monday and tell them you're considering a job offer from them. Ask if they can tell you about things like parking or transit pass discounts. Find out if they might have tuition reimbursements for graduate school courses. See if they can help you understand the benefits a little better."

While parent input is helpful during these job considerations and negotiations, your son or daughter is the one who must fully understand the benefits package and career development opportunities. When it comes to asking specific questions about various costs or benefits, don't make the phone calls for your child, but be a sounding board for questions and concerns.

STUCK BETWEEN COLLEGE AND THE REAL WORLD

Students bring high expectations and lofty goals to college, and as graduating seniors, they will critically reevaluate their plans. Those who have had to lower their expectations face doubt and disillusionment when they have to admit they won't end up where they thought they would. Kanisha had always said she would be an optometrist, but her college grades didn't qualify her for the graduate school she had hoped to attend. "Do I want to get an optometry degree from some school no one has ever heard of? My best grades were in statistics and research practices. Are there research jobs I could do?"

A student's carefully constructed plans can be thrown off track by circumstances beyond his control. Leo was graduating with a teaching certificate just when the state was spiraling into a budget crisis. Teachers were given tentative layoff notices at the start of summer, and Leo couldn't even get a job interview. At every school he contacted, he was advised, "Check back in August. We'll know by then if we'll have any openings."

And sometimes heavy competition for the best jobs requires applicants to sacrifice short-term benefits for the promise of long-term potential. Valerie's double major in organizational communication and human resources qualified her for a promising two-year training program at a Fortune 500 firm, but the company could only tell her that she would be assigned to one of three sites—Phoenix, Minneapolis, or San Francisco. "On the salary they're offering, I could afford to live in Phoenix or Minneapolis," Valerie said, "but if they send me to San Francisco, I'd be living off my credit cards. How do I accept the job without knowing for sure where they're sending me?"

The job search and the decisions that come with it are stressful. To add to the anxiety, just when students are trying to make difficult career or graduate school choices, they're confronting the emotions that come with leaving the first home they've created on their own. The friendships that develop in college are intense. Students feel extremely close to their roommates and study partners, not to mention a boyfriend or girlfriend. Campus is comfortable, professors have become treasured advisers, and now they have to think about leaving it all behind.

Many are simply not ready to face the next steps. They're still busy enjoying college. The idea of leaving school, beginning a career, and trying to be a grown-up seems like a script for a miniseries. It's a cute image, but what does it have to do with reality?

Questioning Carefully

Throughout the senior year, all the relatives and family will be asking, "What are you going to do after you graduate?" "Do you have a job yet?" If students don't have a job lined up, the questions feel like criticisms.

Students respond more positively when the questions are less direct: "Do you think you'll stay in Boston after you graduate?" "What's the job market like for students in your major?"

Questioners will get the update they're looking for, and students won't feel like they're being criticized.

POSTCOLLEGE PARENTING

Some families can afford to support their students after graduation, but many are ready for their sons and daughters to be self-supporting. A few will finance a graduate program, while others believe that postgraduate studies are the student's responsibility. Some will help their adult child buy a condominium, while others can barely afford a graduation gift.

Your son or daughter should be well aware by graduation of the family's financial standing. Any change in levels of support shouldn't come as a surprise. Problems occur when students are unclear about expectations or when they don't know that family circumstances have changed.

For Micah, money had never been an issue. His family owned a successful printing company for three generations, and they had done well. In recent years, though, technology changed the business. As costs for new equipment kept going up, his parents decided to sell out shortly before Micah graduated. In fact, they learned, they probably should have sold the company a decade earlier. They received much less for the sale than they had hoped.

Meanwhile, Micah had planned a postgraduation summer trip to Europe with friends. By August, he was having so much fun that he decided to turn in his plane ticket and extend his trip an extra couple of months. In late October, cold, rainy weather caught up with him in Stockholm, and he called home to ask his parents to put enough money on his debit card for some warm clothes and a plane ticket to Madrid.

He was not expecting his mother's reaction. "You haven't talked to us about any of your plans for months, and now you're calling to ask for *money*? I'll transfer enough for you to come home, but that's it. You know we're on a retirement income. You're twenty-two now, and you need to get a job."

Graduating seniors probably have a sense of the sum of their student loans, but they don't always know what that means in terms of their personal obligations. Elise met with the school's financial aid officer a few weeks before graduation and came away with a printout listing her student loan totals. She called her parents with the news that monthly payments would be $439. Her father said, "You have some time before the first payment is due, right? How are you going to budget for that?"

"Me? What do you mean?" Elise asked. "I thought you were going to make the loan payments. You always said you would pay for college."

"No, Elise. We said we would *help* pay for college," he replied. "And we did. We have parent loans to pay back. Those student loans are your responsibility."

Ideally, parents will have had ongoing discussions about debts, payment plans, and when or how you will help. Items for you to address with your graduating senior:

- How will financial responsibilities change when your student graduates?
- How will college loans be handled? Who pays for what?
- Under what conditions will you help your child financially in the future?

As students begin to support themselves, there will be times when unusual circumstances or your child's own choices put you in the position of deciding whether or not to intervene. A year after she graduated from college, Cassie was working as a news reporter in a midsize city a hundred miles from her family's home. She found a one-bedroom garden apartment in a nice housing complex, and she signed a lease for the red sports coupe she had always wanted. By all appearances, she was doing fine.

When her coworkers asked her to go out for lunch, though, she never ordered anything but a glass of water and a cup of soup. "And can I get extra crackers, please?" she would ask. Conversations with her mother always included hints that she could use some money. With her monthly rent, car payment, and college loan payment, Cassie had nothing left over. She had been a "struggling college student" for four years, and she knew how to stretch every dollar, but she wasn't prepared for this kind of budget constraint. Most frustrating, her credit card debt was mounting, and there was no end in sight.

Parents can find this time of their child's life just as difficult as the college years. "Should we help her out?" Cassie's mother asked her partner. "Maybe we could take over her school loans for a few months. I hate to see her struggle like this."

"We can't be there to bail her out for the rest of her life," her partner said. "We have two other kids to put through college. Cassie could have found a cheaper apartment, and a used car would have been a better choice than that new one. She's got to figure out how to handle her money."

THE RETURN POLICY

You might reach a point when you ask the inevitable question: Should your child move back home? You know it's always there as a backup plan. Many students and parents think that moving home is a logical choice. All the pressure would be off for the student. If there's no rent to pay and no groceries to buy, any salary should be enough to live on. For most students, though, going home is viewed as a temporary fix, an intermediate step while they pay off debts or set aside money for the down payment on a one-bedroom condominium.

Done right, having a graduate move home can be a smart decision for the whole family, but it means a major adjustment for everyone. Parents, siblings, students, and even the family home have changed over four years. People develop new routines and rooms are repurposed. Some suggestions for parents and for students:[24]

---

24. C. A. Petree, "Boomerang Families: Navigating the Parent Role as Students Move Back Home," *AHEPPP Journal* 3, no. 1 (2012): 2–16.

SUGGESTIONS FOR PARENTS

- *Set boundaries for yourself and your adult child.* Remember that it's important to balance lines of authority with mutual respect and independence.
- *Establish expectations about finances.* If you're going to charge rent or ask for contributions to household expenses, clarify the amount, the due date, and consequences if payment is not made.
- *Discuss and divide chores and responsibilities.* Ensure that all family members are contributing to the upkeep of the home. As you develop a new relationship with your graduate, remember that they have experienced a lot and changed significantly while in college. Take advantage of this boomerang period to get to know your student as the adult he or she has become.

SUGGESTIONS FOR STUDENTS

- *Remember that your return home requires an adjustment for parents and siblings,* as well as for you. Be understanding as the family navigates this transition.
- *Living with others brings responsibilities.* Expect to contribute to your parents' home expenses as you would for your own apartment.
- *Remember: You're an adult.* When young adults return home, it's easy to revert to precollege behaviors and patterns. Make a commitment to yourself to maintain your adult status, and when necessary, have calm conversations with your parents about your choices and responsibilities.
- *Establish a plan for next steps.* Finding a job and moving out should be your priorities. Work on those goals daily. Let your parents know you're taking steps

toward your plan, and keep them posted on your progress.

REALITY SHOW: WORK-WORLD EDITION

The routine of a daily job brings home the fact that college was not necessarily the best preparation for life as an adult. Sure, students learned the skills and gained the information they needed to earn a degree and qualify for a job, but adapting to a daily schedule that starts at 8:00 a.m. was not part of the academic lifestyle. The group projects in college courses may have taught teamwork, but they didn't provide preparation for an assistant director who assigns the least desirable tasks and noon-hour coverage of the front desk to the new guy.

College students today are accustomed to incentives and rewards, but their supervisors may be from a generation that expects employees to show up, do their jobs, and not be looking for effusive praise. The special accommodations that recent graduates might view as "no big thing" turn out to be a very big thing to employers focused on the bottom line.

When Kelly received her first performance review, she was pleased when her director pointed out that her work during the previous six months qualified her for a two-and-a-half-percent raise. That evening, though, Kelly did some quick calculations and realized that her raise would hardly be noticeable on her biweekly paycheck. Still, looking at the extra income spread out over the next year, it came out to just about what she needed to pay her auto insurance, which was due in a week.

The next day she asked for a few minutes with her supervisor. "It would really help if I could have my raise in a lump sum now, rather than over the whole year," she explained. "Can I just keep my paycheck the same for the rest of this year, but get the raise all at once? Like, a bonus instead of a raise? I've got this bill I need to pay next week." She couldn't understand why her boss thought she was joking.

Establishing a social life as a college graduate also presents challenges. On a college campus, students are surrounded by young men and women who are all in the same stage of life. Making friends just happens. In the workforce, the person at the next desk might have children to go home to, or be counting the days to retirement. It's hard to establish new relationships at the office, and where do you go as an "adult" to meet someone? The bar scene gets old, talking to someone at the grocery store seems contrived, and after a while, online dating feels desperate.

Once again, parents hear the problems, but your son or daughter needs to come up with the solution. For you, the pangs of parenting will continue, taking both familiar and brand-new forms, no matter how old your child is. If your son takes a new job in a city where he doesn't know anyone, you will worry that he's alone. When your emerging adult moves into a new apartment, you feel a strong urge to visit, or at least see photos. You need a visual image before you can feel entirely comfortable. When something bad happens to your child—a job loss, a breakup, or an illness—you will feel the pain. Remember that well-worn saying about parents being only as happy as their least happy child? It's true. But you will also share the joy and pride of any successes—a new job, a promising relationship, wedding plans, or just a really good day.

If you find yourself wondering whether you're saying and doing the right things for your adult child, you're not alone. The mother of a thirty-year-old doctoral candidate noted, "It's still hard to figure out if she's telling me something because she wants my advice, or if she wants me to listen while she thinks out loud. I always mess that up."

You're not the only mentor your child will have during his life. By the time he leaves college, he'll know he can turn to his favorite professor, a former supervisor, and his college friends for advice and support. College alumni chapters, as well as fraternity and sorority national organizations, link graduates to alumni living all over the world.

Still, your child appreciates you, probably more than you know. Despite all those years when your student deliberately pulled away from family ties, college graduates still want and need their parents' love, support, and approval.

At a graduation reception for student leaders, two seniors were talking about their postcollege plans. Michael was explaining to his friend that he had decided to stay in Minneapolis for law school, turning down acceptances from three other universities.

"I know I'm going to want to live in Minnesota after I get my law degree, so it makes sense to go to school here, do my law internships here, and take the bar in Minnesota."

"Do you really want to stay in Minnesota?" his friend asked. "Don't you want to get away from these winters?"

"Somewhere warm would be nice, but my family is here," Michael said. "I'll admit, sometimes I curse my ancestors for settling in such a cold place, but I know I want to live near my family. Can't help it. I love 'em."

"Yeah, I know what you mean," said his friend, looking at the floor and shuffling awkwardly. "I love my parents, too. It took a while to realize it, but they're about the best people I know."

QUICK TIPS FOR STUDENTS

- For the entire last half of your senior year, people will be asking repeatedly, "What will you do after graduation?" Don't take it personally. Use their question as a networking opportunity. "I'm looking for a job. Do you know of any I might qualify for?"

- Don't think you've failed if you don't have a job lined up before graduation. Summer is a good time to fine-tune the résumé, search job listings, and make sure you have good recommendations from professors or former employers. A lot of jobs open up during the summer. Use the months after graduation to focus on the job hunt, and don't criticize yourself for failing to have something lined up by now.
- It's not a bad idea to take flexible jobs after graduation. You need a job that will allow time off for interviews when they come up.
- Talk with your family about postcollege finances so that you're clear on your obligations and their expectations.
- If your best option after college is to move back home, you have no reason to be embarrassed. If it means you're not racking up more debt, it might be the most rational and responsible choice you can make. But be sure to negotiate boundaries and expectations with your family, then stick to the agreement.
- Tell your parents you appreciate them. They need to hear things like that sometimes.

Appendix A

The Four-Year College Calendar

Each of the college years presents new issues as students develop academic and life skills. Parents may not always know what problems their child is facing at any given time, but some issues are likely to come up during each of the four years of their academic career.

FIRST YEAR

The first year of college is all about change and self-discovery. The critical issues for freshmen are time management, setting limits, and learning new study skills.

Time management: First-year students often struggle to balance studying, socializing, and personal time. All are important. The major goal is to master the academic responsibilities, but it's important to make time for friendships. Students learn more from other students than from classroom lectures, and college provides an opportunity to make friends with young adults from different backgrounds. Students also need time just for themselves. Personal time to exercise, listen to music, or go for a walk allows students to find the energy to handle everything else on their agenda. The occasional quiet hour also gives them a chance to think about how everything they're learning fits with their own value system and personality.

Setting limits: When a little of something brings pleasure, it's hard to know when to stop. During the first weeks of college, students are tempted to stay up too late, sleep too long, party excessively, or even study too much. Balance is critical.

Study skills: The read-and-review or memorization methods that worked in high school are not enough to succeed in college. College classes require that students know how to analyze and think critically about what they're learning. Study skills workshops are available at most colleges, and they're not just for borderline students. Students who are open to finding new ways to study and learn will reap the rewards.

SECOND YEAR

During the second year, students are more comfortable with college. They question themselves less about daily concerns. Nevertheless, students think they should have everything under control, but they know they don't. At the same time, they're starting to internalize their personal values, which often means reassessing relationships. The group of friends from last year is honed to fewer, deeper friendships. All the excitement and challenge of the first year is gone, and the adrenaline rush of transition is missing. This is the traditional sophomore slump.

The critical issues for sophomores involve academic complacency, personal and financial risk, and changing interests and goals.

Academic complacency: During their first year, students learned that they could get by with B's and C's. As sophomores, they're comfortable with turning in average work. They're continuing to fulfill their general education requirements, and it feels like they're biding time until they get into their major. The grades they earn this year, however, can make all the difference when they declare a major or apply for graduate school. Some selective upper-division (junior- and senior-level) programs require a minimum grade point average during the first two years. Graduate schools consider overall undergraduate accomplishments. Some slack may be allowed for first-year adjustment, but students who are lax the second year can lose future opportunities.

Personal and financial risk: Sophomores take risks that they didn't dare to attempt as freshmen and that they won't feel the need to take as juniors. Those who vowed not to drink as first-year students no longer feel so committed to abstinence. This is also a year when financial problems compound. They may have signed up for multiple credit cards as freshmen, but this year they start using them.

Changing interests and goals: All the introductory courses students take during their first two years of college have a purpose. In addition to giving students a strong academic foundation, the courses provide a glimpse of different ways to look at and think about broad subjects. Sophomores are ripe for identifying a passion in life, and they still have time to change their majors.

THIRD YEAR

The junior year can be the best, or it can lead to significant doubts, especially about how the previous two years were spent and whether the next two years can be better. Under ideal circumstances, students are in their major, taking classes that interest them. They know the campus, they have learned the routines, and it feels like life is under control. Juniors are taking leadership positions in campus organizations, and they have friends everywhere they look. Parents worry less about juniors. They can see that their children are making progress. Their students have formally declared a field of study and seem to have a plan for at least the next two years. Like the students, parents have adjusted to the college processes. They know the routine, and they trust their student's ability to handle any problems that come up.

The critical issues for juniors involve disillusionment, regrets, and close relationships.

Disillusionment: Students who are taking advanced classes in their major might be disappointed to find that some of the courses they've been looking forward to are not as exciting as they expected. It can be frustrating for students to acknowledge that they're still learning theory, not applying skills.

Regrets: As juniors, students begin to recognize the consequences of their earlier failures. The C-minus in calculus that felt like a victory two years ago—"At least I passed, and I don't ever have to take another math class!"—now feels like an eternal curse. They try to figure out how they can possibly raise their grade point average to 3.5, and they realize they don't have enough classes left to improve that much. When they look at the three classes they dropped during their first two years in school, they see that there's no way to make up twelve credit hours without committing to another semester on campus. This is also the year when students begin to figure out how much debt they'll have when they graduate. Until now, it was only a meaningless number. Now, as they consider the monthly cost of an apartment and paying off credit card bills, they see how their college debt will affect their postgraduate life.

Close relationships: During childhood, students relied on their family for support and guidance. Throughout the teen years, they increasingly turned to their friends. Now, as they consider the future, they begin to realize that they have to rely on themselves. The close relationships in their lives now feel like a lifeline from the present into an unknown future. Although they know they have plenty of time to find a life partner, it's common for students in their junior year to make long-term promises to their friends and lovers and to feel devastated when a relationship ends.

FOURTH YEAR

Seniors know their niche in school and have made their mark by leading an organization, earning honors for the school, and creating a personal reputation on campus. Just when things should be comfortable, though, they're sweating the next steps. Deadlines come quickly for graduate school exams and applications, and the weight of finding a job hangs over their heads. Families expect students to have a solid plan in mind.

The critical issues for seniors involve balancing priorities, racing against time, and facing the unknown.

Balancing priorities: Students who neglected to take all their required lower-division courses must complete them before they can graduate. They're annoyed to be spending time on freshman-level classes, but they have to fulfill the requirements. Meanwhile, they have senior papers or major projects due. Every new assignment seems to get in the way of a previous commitment.

Race against time: The college career that once seemed to stretch way into the future is now boiled down to eight short months. When fall semester begins, seniors already feel as if they're behind schedule. If their next step is graduate school, they should have narrowed down their selections by now. In short order, they must take the Graduate Record Exam or professional school tests, and it takes time to write a compelling grad school application. Students who will be looking for a job need to be polishing a résumé and researching possible job openings.

Facing the unknown: With the end of school in sight, students begin to fear the blank slate in front of them. If they plan to move to another area, they'll be leaving everything that's familiar. They're not just finding a new job or enrolling in a new school, they'll also be looking for a new apartment, meeting new people, and starting new routines. They'll be expected to make payments on educational loans. Even if they're staying in the same town, life will change.

Appendix B

Vocabulary of Higher Education

*E*very college and university has its own unique terminology. If you don't find the term or phrase you're looking for on this list, contact your student's school to ask for a definition.

ACADEMICS

Academic adviser: A staff or faculty member who provides academic advice to students to guide them through the requirements for earning a college degree. Academic advisers can also provide guidance on personal and career issues.

Adjunct faculty: Faculty members who are hired to teach a specific class; often these are part-time instructors who have full-time jobs in the field they're teaching.

Advanced Placement (AP): Academically challenging courses taken during high school that prepare students for challenging examinations in the course subjects. If students achieve a specific score on the tests, a college or university may grant college credits for the courses.

Associate degree: A college degree that requires less than four years of full-time college study; it usually takes two years of full-time study to earn an associate degree. The associate degree can transfer to a four-year school with credits fulfilling requirements toward a four-year bachelor's degree.

Auditing: Registering for a course in order to attend classes without receiving credit or grades.

Bachelor's degree: Also called a baccalaureate degree, this degree is awarded for the equivalent of four years of full-time college work.

Commencement: College graduation ceremony.

Community service/Service learning: Learning experiences that take students out of the classroom to apply their education in the community. A service learning experience should include active participation along with critical reflection under the guidance of an instructor or supervisor.

Convocation: A campus-wide gathering. The term typically applies to a celebration at the beginning of the academic year.

Credit or credit hour: College courses are generally described in terms of the number of hours of instruction per week. Students qualify for graduation by earning a specified number of credits, which apply to a major or minor and fulfill required areas of study.

Curve grading: Awarding grades on the overall performance of students in the class. The student with the most questions answered correctly receives an A; the student with the fewest right answers fails. Instructors base the scale on a "bell curve," awarding the majority of students a C, with fewer students receiving A's and F's and those in between receiving B's or D's.

Dean's list: High-achieving students who have earned a specified overall grade point average during a term. The list is issued by the dean of the college or department.

Distance learning: College courses are offered through broadcast or online instruction or by correspondence. A portion of the coursework may include on-campus meetings.

Double major: Students can elect to fulfill the graduation requirements of two majors.

Early-action admission: An application process that allows students to apply and be notified of an admission decision before the school's regular notification dates. Under early action, a student is not obligated to attend the institution. In some cases, students can apply to more than one early-action school.

Early-decision admission: An application process that notifies students of an admission decision much earlier than the regular admission deadline. Students who apply under this plan must commit to attend the institution if they are accepted.

Elective: A course that a student may choose to take, but that is not among the courses required for the student's major.

Family Educational Rights and Privacy Act (FERPA): A federal law that protects the privacy of student educational records. At the college level, this law stipulates that authority over student records belongs to the student. See www.ed.gov /policy/gen/guid/fpco/ferpa/index.html.

General Education Requirements (also called Liberal Education Requirements and Core Curriculum): A foundation of coursework that introduces students to a wide range of disciplines and teaches a standard set of competencies. These courses typically emphasize communication skills, critical thinking and analysis, and civic engagement.

Grade point average (GPA): The numerical average of a student's grades for the semester or for the entire college record. The GPA is determined by converting the letter grade for the course to a number (A = 4, B = 3, C = 2, D = 1, and F = 0); multiplying the numerical grade by the number of credits for that course; totaling the scores for all courses; then dividing by the overall number of credit hours earned.

Incomplete: A grade registered on the student's transcript indicating the student has not met all the requirements of the course. An incomplete is considered a temporary grade; if the class is not completed within a specified time, the incomplete becomes an F.

Independent study: A course designed under the direction of a faculty member, usually providing more specific investigation of a topic than is offered in a traditional college course. This type of class may be designed for an individual student or a small number of students.

Internship: A work opportunity allowing students to practice professional skills in a supervised setting. Internships may be offered with or without pay and with or without college credit.

Learning center or **learning commons:** A center on campus providing assistance in academic areas or study skills. It may include tutoring, online resources, or workshops. Assistance is offered in such areas as reading, writing, math, and sciences, as well as note taking, studying, time management, and test taking.

Major: An academic area that a student chooses as a primary field of study. A certain number of credits are required to be earned within the major in order to graduate.

Master's degree: A degree requiring the equivalent of one or two additional years of study after the bachelor's or undergraduate degree. In a master's program, students focus on a field of study in greater detail.

Minor: An academic area that a student may choose to take several classes in (typically five). A minor can complement a student's major, emphasizing a second area of interest. It does not require as many credit hours as a major but may require the student to attend school an extra semester.

Orientation: An introduction to college life. Orientation programs are common for new students, and many colleges and universities also offer orientation programs for parents and families, for international students, and for commuters and transfer students. The programs generally address academic, social, and emotional aspects of starting college, and students frequently register for their first semester's classes at orientation.

Pass/Fail: A system of grading that does not award letter or numerical grades but indicates whether a student has completed the coursework sufficiently to pass.

Portfolio: A collection of student work that presents examples of papers or projects. It allows students to present examples of their work and to reflect on their knowledge and abilities.

Prerequisite: A course that must be completed before a student is allowed to register for a more advanced course or to qualify for a program or major.

Probation: A designation indicating that a student's work is not satisfactory. A set of conditions is imposed for students to improve performance by a designated time. Failure to meet the conditions will result in expulsion from the school or the program.

Registration: The process of selecting and enrolling in courses.

Rolling admission: The process of reviewing and making decisions on admission applications as they arrive rather than enforcing application deadlines after which no further decisions will be made.

Semester/Trimester: The academic calendar is broken into terms of study. Schools are either on a semester system, with two semesters making up a year of study, or a trimester system, where the academic year is divided into three periods of study. Some schools refer to "quarters" when an academic year is divided into four parts, with summer session considered one of the four.

Seminar: A small class, usually focused on a specialized topic that relies heavily on discussions rather than lectures.

Study abroad: A program in which students earn college credit while studying in another country. Programs may be one or two weeks, a summer, a full semester, or an entire year.

Syllabus: An outline and description of a course, usually handed out on the first day of class. The syllabus provides contact information for the instructor and office hours. It describes the instructor's expectations for the course and gives an overview of the topics covered; required and recommended readings; grading policies; and a schedule of tests and due dates for papers or projects.

Transcript: A list of courses the student has taken, grades for each course, and the number of credits earned. The transcript is the formal record of a student's education. Upon graduation, it will reflect the successful completion of a degree from the institution.

Tuition: The cost charged to take courses. Tuition is only one part of the college bill; students will also be billed for fees (including technology fees, student services fees, and sometimes separate course fees), and those who live on campus are charged for room and board to cover residence halls and dining expenses. Other costs may not be included on the college billing but are still required, such as books and supplies.

Withdrawal: An official process for dropping out of a class or leaving the institution without completing requirements for a degree.

FINANCES

Cost of attendance: The estimated cost for attending school for a year. The cost of attendance includes tuition and fees, books, supplies, room and board, transportation, and an estimate of other personal costs.

Family contribution: An estimate from the college or university of the amount the family is expected to pay toward a student's cost of attendance. A student contribution designates how much the student is expected to contribute.

Financial need: The difference between the cost of attendance and how much the student will need in financial aid. The amount is broken down to reflect scholarships, grants, loans, and student jobs.

FAFSA or Free Application for Federal Student Aid: A process of the U.S. Department of Education for the purpose of collecting the information used to determine a student's need for federal financial aid. See https://studentaid.ed.gov/sa/fafsa/.

Grant: Financial aid that does not have to be repaid.

Work-study: Student jobs funded through the U.S. government's Federal Work-Study Program. Work-study positions allow students to work on or near campus in order to help pay their college expenses. Work-study funds are packaged into a student's financial aid award. The number of hours a student may work during the semester or the year is specified in the award.

PEOPLE

Board of directors or board of trustees: The decision-making group that oversees the college or university. This group sets policies, establishes budgets, and delegates the day-to-day running of the institution to an administrator, such as a president or chancellor, and to academic officers.

Board of regents: State colleges and universities may be run by a board of regents whose members are approved by the state legislature. This board functions much as a board of directors or trustees.

Bursar: The university official or the office where bills and fees are paid.

Chancellor: The senior administrator of an institution or a higher-education system. At some schools, the senior administrator holds the title of president.

Chief Academic Officer (CAO): The administrator who oversees the academic responsibilities of a college or university. In some schools this position is called Provost, Academic Dean, Dean of Faculty, or Vice President of Academic Affairs.

Dean: Colleges and universities are divided into major administrative units, and a dean is the head of one of those units. There may be a dean of Liberal Arts, Mathematics and Sciences, Library and Information Services, the graduate school, and a dean of students.

Full-time student: A student who is taking a full load of college credits during the semester or trimester. Typically, a full-time undergraduate student is registered for at least twelve credits during a semester. Taking fewer credits than full-time status can affect a student's eligibility for financial aid, academic scholarships, and honors.

Provost: See *Chief Academic Officer.*

Registrar: The official or the office responsible for coordinating class registration and for maintaining educational records at the college or university.

Research assistant/Teaching assistant: A graduate student who works part-time as an assistant to a faculty member. Undergraduates may also have an assistantship at some schools.

Resident assistant/Resident adviser: An upperclassman or graduate student living in a residence hall and serving as an adviser to students. In some colleges, the title might be Community Adviser, Hall Fellow, or some other designation, and titles are usually abbreviated to RA, CA, etc. RAs undergo extensive training to ensure that institutional policies and procedures are followed. They help residents with roommate conflicts and provide guidance related to the college experience, and they organize social activities for their residents.

Transfer student: A student who has attended college and earned credits and later enrolls at another college or university.

Selected Bibliography

Abel, J. R., and R. Deitz. "Despite Rising Costs, College Is Still a Good Investment." Liberty Street Economics, June 5, 2019. https://www.cnbc.com/2017/10/04/students-who-work-actually-get-better-grades-but-theres-a-catch.html.

American College Health Association. American College Health Association—National College Health Assessment II: Reference Group Executive Summary Spring 2018. Silver Spring, MD: American College Health Association, 2019. https://www.acha.org/documents/ncha/NCHA-II_Spring_2018_Reference_Group_Executive_Summary.pdf (accessed June 17, 2019).

Anxiety and Depression Association of America. "Facts and Statistics." https://adaa.org/about-adaa/press-room/facts-statistics (accessed July 23, 2019).

Arnett, J. J., and J. L. Tanner. *Emerging Adults in America: Coming of Age in the 21st Century*. Washington, DC: American Psychological Association, 2006.

Astin, A.W., and G. Erlandson. *Four Critical Years Revisited*. San Francisco: Jossey-Bass, 1997.

Bowlby, J. *A Secure Base: Parent-Child Attachment and Healthy Human Development*. New York: Basic Books, 1988.

Breland, A. "If the Tuition Doesn't Get You, the Cost of Housing Will." *Bloomberg BusinessWeek*, August 13, 2019. https://www.bloomberg.com/news/features/2019-08-13/if-the-tuition-doesn-t-get-you-the-cost-of-student-housing-will (accessed August 13, 2019).

Buhl, H. M., P. Noack, and B. Kracke. "The Role of Parents and Peers in the

Transition from University to Work Life." *Journal of Career Development* 45, no. 6 (2018): 523–35.

Carlson, C. L. "Seeking Self-Sufficiency: Why Emerging Adult College Students Receive and Implement Parental Advice." *Emerging Adulthood* 2, no. 4 (2014): 257–69.

Carney-Hall, K. C., ed. *Managing Parent Partnerships: Maximizing Influence, Minimizing Interference, and Focusing on Student Success.* San Francisco: Jossey-Bass New Directions for Student Services, 2008.

Centers for Disease Control and Prevention. Alcohol and Public Health Fact Sheet. https://www.cdc.gov/alcohol/fact-sheets/minimum-legal-drinking-age.htm (accessed July 15, 2019).

Chickering, A. W., and L. Reisser. *Education and Identity.* San Francisco: Jossey-Bass.

Dworak, S. "Fake IDs in America: Challenges of Identification and the Critical Need for Training." Real Identities LLC, 2018. https://www.centerforalcoholpolicy.org/wp-content/uploads/2018/07/FAKE-IDs-IN-AMERICA-2018.pdf (accessed August 11, 2019).

Edwards, T., J. C. Catling, and E. Parry. "Identifying Predictors of Resilience in Students." *Psychology Teaching Review* 1 (2016): 26–34.

Francis, G. L., J. Duke, F. J. Brigham, and K. Demetro. "Student Perceptions of College-Readiness, College Services and Supports, and Family Involvement in College: An Exploratory Study." *Journal of Autism and Developmental Disorders* 48 (2018): 3573–85.

Fry, R. "Early Benchmarks Show Post-Millennials on Track to Be Most Diverse, Best-Educated Generation Yet." Pew Research, 2018. https://www.pewsocialtrends.org/2018/11/15/early-benchmarks-show-post-millennials-on-track-to-be-most-diverse-best-educated-generation-yet/ (accessed December 20, 2018).

Hess, A. "Students Who Work Actually Get Better Grades—but There's a Catch." CNBC Make It, October 5, 2017. https://www.cnbc.com/2017/10/04/students-who-work-actually-get-better-grades-but-theres-a-catch.html (accessed August 15, 2019).

Hillier, A., et al. "Supporting University Students with Autism Spectrum Disorder." *Autism,* 22, no. 1 (2018): 2–28.

Howard, J. M., B. C. Nicholson, and S. R. Chesnut. "Relationships Between

Positive Parenting, Overparenting, Grit, and Academic Success." *Journal of College Student Development* 60, no. 2 (2019): 189–202.

Johnston, L. D., et al. *Monitoring the Future: National Survey Results on Drug Use 1975–2018*. Ann Arbor: Institute for Social Research, University of Michigan, 2019. http://www.monitoringthefuture.org//pubs/monographs/mtf-overview2018.pdf (accessed July 15, 2019).

Kafka, A. C. "How Some Colleges Are Helping Freshmen Find Their Academic Focus." *Chronicle of Higher Education,* August 11, 2019.

Kelly, J. "Unpopular Advice People Are Too Afraid to Give to New College Graduates and Their Parents." *Forbes,* May 10, 2019. https://www.forbes.com/sites/jackkelly/2019/05/10/unpopular-advice-people-are-too-afraid-to-give-new-college-graduates-and-their-parents/#18fe1d10499e (accessed May 10, 2019).

Light, R. *Making the Most of College: Students Speak Their Minds*. Cambridge, MA: Harvard University Press, 2004.

Lowe, K., and A. M. Dotterer. "Parental Involvement During the College Transition: A Review and Suggestion for Its Conceptual Definition." *Adolescent Research Review* 3 (2018): 29–42.

Maslow, A. *The Farther Reaches of Human Nature*. New York: Viking, 1971.

NACE. "Career Readiness Defined." https://www.naceweb.org/career-readiness/competencies/career-readiness-defined/.

Nadworny, E. "College Completion Rates Are Up, but the Numbers Will Still Surprise You." National Public Radio, March 13, 2019. https://www.npr.org/2019/03/13/681621047/college-completion-rates-are-up-but-the-numbers-will-still-surprise-you (accessed March 15, 2019).

National Center for Education Statistics. Fast Facts. https://nces.ed.gov/fastfacts/display.asp?id=31 (accessed August 22, 2019).

National Sexual Violence Resource Center. Campus Sexual Assault. https://www.nsvrc.org/node/4737 (accessed August 23, 2019).

Newman, B. M., and P. R. Newman. *Development Through Life: A Psychosocial Approach*. N.p.: Wadsworth, 2017.

O'Keefe, P. A., C. S. Dweck, and G. M. Walton. "Implicit Theories of Interest: Finding Your Passion or Developing It?" http://gregorywalton-stanford.weebly.com/uploads/4/9/4/4/49448111/okeefedweckwalton_2018.pdf (accessed August 1, 2019).

Pascarella, E. T., and P. T. Terenzini. *How College Affects Students: A Third Decade of Research*. San Francisco: Jossey-Bass, 2005.

Petree, C. A. "Boomerang Families: Navigating the Parent Role as Students Move Back Home." *AHEPPP Journal* 3, no. 1 (2012): 2–16.

———. "Parents' and Graduates' Perspectives on the Challenges and Benefits to Boomerang Families." *AHEPPP Journal* 3, no. 2 (2012): 20–33.

Rusby, J. C., J. M. Light, R. Crowley, and E. Westling. "Influence of Parent-Youth Relationship, Parental Monitoring, and Parent Substance Use on Adolescent Substance Use Onset." *Journal of Family Psychology* 32, no. 3 (2017): 310–20.

Schulenberg, J. E., L. D. Johnston, P. M. O'Malley, J. G. Bachman, R. A. Miech, and M. E. Patrick. *Monitoring the Future: National Survey Results on Drug Use, 1975–2017*, vol. 2, *College Students and Adults Ages 19–55*. Ann Arbor: Institute for Social Research, University of Michigan, 2019.

Seemiller, C., and M. Grace. *Generation Z Goes to College*. San Francisco: Wiley, 2016.

Shapiro, D., et al. *Transfer and Mobility: A National View of Student Movement in Postsecondary Institutions, Fall 2011 Cohort*. Signature Report No. 15, Herndon, VA: National Student Clearinghouse Research Center, 2018.

Sokol, B. W., F. M. E. Grouzet, and U. Müller. *Self-Regulation and Autonomy: Social and Developmental Dimensions of Human Conduct*. New York: Cambridge University Press, 2013.

Temmen, C. D., and L. J. Crockett. "Adolescent Predictors of Social and Coping Drinking Motives in Early Adulthood." *Journal of Adolescence* 66 (2018): 1–8.

United States Department of Education. "Programs: Family Educational Rights and Privacy Act." https://www2.ed.gov/policy/gen/guid/fpco /ferpa/index.html (accessed July 14, 2019).

United States Department of Health and Human Services. "FERPA and HIPAA." https://www2.ed.gov/policy/gen/guid/fpco/doc/ferpa-hipaa -guidance.pdf (accessed July 14, 2019).

United States Government Accountability Office. *Higher Education: Students Need More Information to Help Reduce Challenges in Transferring College Credits*. 2017. https://www.gao.gov/assets/690/686530.pdf (accessed January 20, 2019).

Van Hees, V., H. Roeyers, and J. De Mol. "Students with Autism Spectrum

Disorder and Their Parents in the Transition into Higher Education: Impact on Dynamics in the Parent-Child Relationship." *Journal of Autism and Developmental Disorders* 48 (2018): 3296–3310.

Waithaka, A. G., T. M. Furniss, and P. N. Gitimu. "College Student Mind-set: Does Student-Parental Relationship Influence the Student's Mind-set?" *Research in Higher Education Journal* 32 (2017). https://files.eric.ed.gov /fulltext/EJ1148938.pdf (accessed July 28, 2019).

Weissbourd, R. *Turning the Tide II: How Parents and High Schools Can Cultivate Ethical Character and Reduce Distress in the College Admissions Process.* Harvard Graduate School of Education, 2019. https://static1.square space.com/static/5b7c56e255b02c683659fe43/t/5d0ce3d3b35b4b0001 d0e443/1561125854274/TTT2+FINAL+2019.pdf (accessed August 20, 2019).

Ziemniak, A. "The Contribution of Family Members to First Generation College Student Success." *AHEPPP Journal* 3 (2011): 12–26.

Index

Marjorie Savage is an education specialist in the Department of Family Social Science at the University of Minnesota, where she researches parenting college students (https://innovation.umn .edu/college-parent/). She lives in Inver Grove Heights, Minnesota.